find
your
light

find your light

Practicing Mindfulness
to Recover from Anything

BEVERLY CONYERS

Hazelden
Publishing

Hazelden Publishing
Center City, Minnesota 55012
hazelden.org/bookstore

Library of Congress Cataloging-in-Publication Data

Names: Conyers, Beverly, author.

Title: Find your light : practicing mindfulness to recover from anything /
  Beverly Conyers.

Description: First Edition. | Center City, Minnesota : Hazelden Publishing,
  [2019] | Includes bibliographical references.

Identifiers: LCCN 2019026140 (print) | LCCN 2019026141 (ebook) | ISBN
  9781616498030 (trade paperback) | ISBN 9781616498047 (ebook)

Subjects: LCSH: Mindfulness (Psychology) | Self-actualization (Psychology)

Classification: LCC BF637.M56 C66 2019 (print) | LCC BF637.M56 (ebook) |
  DDC 158.1/3--dc23

LC record available at https://lccn.loc.gov/2019026140

LC ebook record available at https://lccn.loc.gov/2019026141

Editor's notes

The names, details, and circumstances have been changed to protect the privacy
of those mentioned in this publication.

This publication is not intended as a substitute for the advice of health care
professionals.

Readers should be aware that websites listed in this work may have changed or
disappeared between when this work was written and when it is read.

Alcoholics Anonymous, AA, and the Big Book are registered trademarks of
Alcoholics Anonymous World Services, Inc.

In chapter 1, Present Light, The Twelve Steps come from *Alcoholics Anonymous*,
4th ed., (New York: Alcoholics Anonymous World Services, 2001), pages 59–60.

In chapter 3, Enlightened Self-Awareness, "Saint Francis and the Sow" comes from
Mortal Acts, Mortal Words by Galway Kinnell. Copyright © 1990, renewed 2008 by
Galway Kinnell. Reprinted by permission of Houghton Mifflin Harcourt Publishing
Company. All rights reserved.

24 23 22 21 20   1 2 3 4 5 6

Cover and interior design: Terri Kinne
Acquisitions editor: Vanessa Torrado
Development editors: Mindy Keskinen and Vanessa Torrado
Editorial project manager: Jean Cook

*

For Jessica, Cullen, Sonya, and Marjorie
—you light up my life

*

Contents

Introduction: What Now?   1

Why Mindfulness? 3

1. Present Light   7

Finding the Light 8
What Do You Intend? 11
Less Impulse, More Intention 15
The Power of Non-Doing 16
Just Breathe 20
Mindfulness and the Twelve Steps 21
From Powerlessness to Mindfulness 26

2. Waking Up   29

Thoughts and Awareness: What's the Difference? 31
Shedding Light on Our Preconceptions 33
Adjusting Your Default Setting: Avoiding Five Mental Traps 36
Seeing without Judging 41
Clarity through Humility 46

3. Enlightened Self-Awareness   51

What Is Happiness? 53
Enlightened Self-Awareness 56
A Fresh Take on a "Fearless Moral Inventory" 59
The Stories We Tell Ourselves 63
What Shame, Guilt, and Anger Can Teach Us 67
The One We Feed 72

4. The Healing Light of Compassion   75

Why Is There So Much Suffering? 76
Finding Meaning in Pain 79
What's Compassion Got to Do with It? 82
Difficult Relationships 85
Choosing Forgiveness 88
Why Self-Compassion Matters 92

5. The Beacon of Virtue   99

The Values-Happiness Connection 101
Lighting a Moral Path 103
The Eightfold Path 107
Freedom through Self-Discipline 111
What about Karma? 115

6. An Illuminated Life   119

A Power Greater Than Ourselves 120
The Illusion of Separateness 123
The Eternal in the Here and Now 127
Having Had a Spiritual Awakening 129
Rediscovering Joy 131

Afterword: Lightening Up   135

Acknowledgments 139
Resources 141
Notes 143
About the Author 149

What Now?

Whether this book has come to you as a gift or whether you purposely sought it out, you are likely trying to heal or regain an important aspect of your life. In other words, you are a person in *recovery* from an activity, behavior, or substance that has had a damaging impact on your personal well-being. You are not alone. Nowadays, it can seem like almost everyone is in recovery from something. Maybe that's because there's a lot to recover from in this world.

Changing social norms, fast-paced lifestyles, and constant information and access to anything and everything have all contributed to increased levels of stress, anxiety, and depression. Many of us grapple with social isolation or fragile support networks while also trying to come to terms with past traumas or difficult family dynamics. Easily developed and triggered compulsions—which at first may seem to offer relief—can quickly devolve into self-sabotaging behaviors like substance use or disordered eating, codependency or workaholism, gambling or compulsive internet use, porn or sex addiction, or other habitual patterns of escape.

As people in recovery, we take justifiable pride in the progress we've made. We've established our hard-earned abstinence from alcohol or other drugs. Or we've found healthy replacements for the reflexive behaviors that once consumed our life. Maybe we've worked on our personal growth and found new, productive ways to cope with life's challenges. *And yet . . .*

And yet, the questions start to nag at us: *What now? Is this all there is?*

Somehow, we'd imagined that recovery would make us happier. More satisfied. More *content*. We'd hoped it would transform us into a new and improved version of ourselves, vanquishing the doubts and unhappiness that helped fuel our compulsions in the first place. Instead, what we often find as our recovery unfolds is that we still have a lot of work to do. Many of the old demons are still there.

In a way, that's not surprising. After all, addiction—which in this book refers to *any* unhealthy personal compulsion from which we're recovering—not only *masked* our problems. It *intensified* them. It stunted our social skills and prevented us from dealing with trauma and other emotional sticking points. It kept us from nurturing our strengths and developing our talents.

Most damaging of all, our compulsions diverted us from the fundamental task of learning about our *self*—that unique and precious being who is like no other on the planet. Having a secure sense of self is essential to personal happiness. Yet the search for identity is almost always a complicated process. Any pattern of avoidance, addiction, or compulsion makes it even harder.

None of us comes into the world knowing who we are. Instead, we build our personal identity through a long process of trial and error—discovering our likes and dislikes, testing our strengths and weaknesses, exploring our dreams and fears in a changing world. Because compulsive behaviors numb the thoughts, feelings, and insights that lead us to who we are, they shut the door on self-discovery.

Opening that door is the very heart of recovery. In its deepest sense, recovery involves much more than freeing ourselves from the damaging grip of addictive substances and behaviors. It means reconnecting with—or discovering for the first time—what gives meaning and purpose to our life. And that becomes clear only when we know, accept, and value who we really are.

Mindfulness can light the way on this complex journey of self-discovery.

Why Mindfulness?

Introduced by the Buddha as a path to spiritual enlightenment more than twenty-five hundred years ago, mindfulness is the art of being fully present, moment to moment, in our lives. Because addiction is in many respects a disease of avoidance, of *not* being present, mindfulness is especially helpful for those of us who are in recovery from any kind of compulsive problematic behavior.

Among its many benefits, mindfulness teaches us how to live *intentionally*—to consciously direct our choices and actions in ways that bring a greater sense of contentment. It also teaches us

- to quiet racing thoughts and manage difficult emotions
- to weather life's ups and downs with equanimity
- to replace the darkness of shame with the healing light of self-compassion
- to let go of painful feelings of separateness and connect meaningfully with others
- to awaken our innate capacity to experience joy.

And—by freeing our mind from the constant noise and distractions of daily life—mindfulness clears a quiet space in which to discover our own inner truths.

For me, mini-mindfulness practices throughout the day have helped me control my codependent tendencies and improved my relationships with the people I love. A relative who meditates daily said that "taking just ten minutes every morning to focus my mind keeps me from getting stuck in those negative thoughts that could make me pick up a drink." And a friend's son told me that the mindfulness training he received while in treatment for opioid addiction has "helped me overcome the shame I felt about my addiction. It's easier to stay clean when you don't feel bad about yourself."

Think about those statements for a moment. What patterns are keeping you feeling stuck? What limitations are you applying to your everyday journey? Are there ways you have continued to sabotage yourself? Do lifestyle patterns, self-doubt, or roles you play with people you encounter regularly keep you feeling as though you are less than everything around you? If your answer to any of these questions is *yes,* then you are likely still hoping to find or reclaim something of your *self.* You are hoping not just to journey in recovery, but to *thrive* in recovery.

This book invites you to explore how mindfulness can help you to do just that. Although compatible with the Twelve Step programs that are so helpful to many people in recovery, it can illuminate any recovery path. After all, everyone's journey is different. There is no "one size fits all" when it comes to personal growth.

In each chapter, you'll find suggestions for practice and reflection, but keep in mind they are merely that: suggestions. You are your own best teacher. Use what works for you and set aside the rest. You may wish to experiment with mindfulness only in brief, informal moments. You may choose to explore it through journaling or other creative practices. Or you may decide to deepen a mindfulness practice through formal meditation. This book offers you all those options.

Whatever path you choose, the ancient art of mindfulness can illuminate your path to a richer, more meaningful recovery and a happier way of life.

●

Present Light

Look to this day!
For it is life, the very life of life.
In its brief course
Lie all the verities and realities of your existence:
The bliss of growth,
The glory of action,
The splendor of beauty.
For yesterday is but a dream
And tomorrow is only a vision.
But today, well-lived,
Makes every yesterday a dream of happiness
And every tomorrow a vision of hope.
Look well, therefore, to this day.
Such is the salutation of the dawn.

—Kalidasa, translated from Sanskrit

IN A WAY, mindfulness and addiction are like day and night.

Mindfulness teaches us to wake up to the present moment. It promotes a state of compassionate awareness in which we know and value our inner self and become conscious participants in our own life. With the practice of mindfulness, we open our eyes to the true nature of reality and learn how to live in harmony with the world around us.

Any kind of addiction, on the other hand, clouds awareness. It distorts reality and prevents us from connecting with others in any meaningful way. When we numb ourselves with compulsive behaviors or addictive substances, we enter a twilight realm in which reality is temporarily suspended. We lose touch not only with the outer world, but with our innermost thoughts and feelings. We come to exist as if in a trance, distracted by fleeting sensations and disconnected from our own inner being.

This is hardly earth-shattering news. After all, oblivion is exactly what many of us were looking for. We wanted to silence the frightening thoughts and feelings, to hide from the overwhelming problems, and to run from the emptiness inside. When our compulsions were active, the last thing we wanted was to "get in touch with" our inner self. Who knew what dreadful things we might find there? How could we handle a reality that seemed too awful to face?

Finding the Light

Recovery shines a light of clarity through the fog of fear and confusion. But even in recovery, our long love affair with escapism can make it hard to embrace the notion of being mindful. We're not alone. As Merle in the hit TV drama *The Walking Dead* illustrates, it's easy to go through life in a quasi-conscious fog:

> Rick: "Do you even know why you do the things you do, the choices you make?"
>
> Merle: "I don't know why I do the things I do. Never did. I'm a damn mystery to me."
>
> —*The Walking Dead,* season 3

Like Merle, many of us are a mystery to ourselves. We don't understand what makes us tick or why we do what we do. Instead, we go about our days doing the same things and thinking the same thoughts, carried along on a tide of seeming inevitability as if we have no choice in the matter. We develop fixed ideas about who we are, fixed notions about what we can and can't do, fixed patterns of reacting to people and situations—all without ever stopping to ask ourselves if we're happy or if what we believe is even true.

It's almost like we've been put on autopilot, seemingly awake but seldom fully aware of who we are and what we're doing. We become passive observers of our own lives.

Technology has only worsened this tendency toward quasi-consciousness. Look around and you'll see an entire society caught up in perpetual distractions. Our screens instantly transport us to places other than where we actually *are.* We check social media, start a game, or switch on the TV, and before we know it, hours have flown by—hours in which we've had no conscious contact with ourselves or our surroundings.

So accustomed are we to the mesmerizing distractions at our fingertips that the notion of simply *being in the present moment* can seem burdensome. A study published in the July 2014 online journal *Science* bore this out: when given a choice between sitting alone quietly for fifteen minutes or giving themselves an electric shock, 25 percent of the female and 67 percent of the male participants chose to shock themselves.

Think about it. Left alone with no devices to occupy their minds, a wide swath of ordinary adults chose an electric shock over stillness. But as startling as this might seem, it's not entirely surprising.

The truth is, it's hard for most of us to pay attention to the present moment. Unless we're engaged in something that's personally meaningful—a challenging problem, useful work, stimulating conversation, a captivating novel or piece of music—our mind tends to go on autopilot. (Think of all the times you've driven from point A to point B, only to arrive with little recollection of how you got there.) Or we look for diversions. This is completely normal. The human brain naturally fluctuates between varying states of attentiveness. It would be exhausting, and likely impossible, for most of us to be fully aware and engaged all the time. We *need* a mental break!

The problem occurs when we spend *most* of our waking hours in a quasi-conscious fog, tuned out and distanced from the reality of our own lives. Days, weeks, months, and even years can fly by in a blur, until one day we stop and ask ourselves where it all went. As people in recovery, we're not immune to the lure of a quasi-conscious existence. Our desire to live a sober, more thoughtful life doesn't protect us from slipping into a life of diminished awareness—from taking the path of least resistance.

Mindfulness offers a different path.

When we choose to be awake and present in the actual moments of our daily lives, we begin to grow in unexpected ways. We learn to let go of harmful, often deep-rooted misperceptions about our self and others. We gain a deeper appreciation of our strengths and values. We expand our capacity for love and connection. And we lay the foundation for a more contented, more meaningful life. Becoming more mindful, like the pursuit of any worthwhile goal, requires intention, self-discipline, and practice. Most of all, it requires the willingness to open our hearts and minds to a new way of experiencing the world.

> **REFLECTION:** "Look to this day! For it is life, the very life of life." More than fifteen hundred years ago, the Indian poet Kalidasa urged us to live each day to the best of our ability. *How can you live to the best of your ability today?*

What Do You Intend?

What kind of day do you intend to have when you wake up tomorrow? What do you intend to happen as a result of an upcoming conversation with a relative or coworker? How do you intend your next meal to affect your health and well-being?

Questions like these don't come naturally for most of us as we go about our daily routine. Yet the simple act of pausing to think about a desired outcome *before we act* can have a powerful impact on the quality of our life.

Consider the role of intent in an ordinary day. Most of us start with some kind of agenda in mind: I'll drop off the kids at school, plug away at that project at work, pick up some groceries on the way home, and catch up on my favorite TV show later on. If we haven't paused to consider our deeper, more heartfelt intent before each of these actions, we're likely to proceed in an automated way. We'll get things done, but our attention will seldom be fully engaged. By the time we fall into bed at night, the day will have sped by, leaving scarcely a trace. It will soon blend in with all the others that have faded over the years.

If, on the other hand, we've taken a moment to think about our intent beforehand, we might give our children an extra hug before dropping them off, to let them know how much we love them. We might risk suggesting a new approach to that work project. We might try adding a nutritious vegetable to our family meal. And we might decide to thoroughly enjoy our favorite TV show with no distractions. Or we might choose to take a walk instead.

The point is, intention can awaken us to the often-overlooked truth that in all the moments of our daily life, we have the power of choice: we can choose to pay attention to what really matters to us.

In his essay "Papa the Educator," author Leo Buscaglia recalls a nightly ritual at the family dinner table:

> Papa, at the head of the table, would push his chair back slightly, a gesture that signified the end of the eating and suggested that there would be a new activity. He would pour a small glass of red wine, light up a thin, potent Italian cigar, inhale deeply, exhale, then take stock of his family.

For some reason this always had a slightly unset-
tling effect on us as we stared back at Papa, waiting
for him to say something. Every so often he would
explain why he did this. He told us that if he didn't
take time to look at us, we would soon be grown
and he would have missed us.

What a wise man! Buscaglia's father wanted the family meal to
be more than simply a time to eat. He intended it to be a time to
fully see and appreciate his children. In these moments of mindful
engagement, his children were nurtured and family bonds were
strengthened.

For most of us, intention is the springboard to mindfulness.
When we *intend* to live with greater awareness and purpose, we
begin to wake up to the thoughts and behaviors that shape our life.

If you've ever spent time with small children, you've wit-
nessed their instinctive fascination with the simplest of things. A
fallen leaf, a rock, a set of keys—all are worthy of close scrutiny.
Their curiosity is boundless, and while their attention span may
be short, they are nevertheless eager to learn about everything
they see. But on the journey to adulthood, we lose much of that
ability to be fully engaged in the moment. Our mind fills with re-
sponsibilities and obligations. We obsess about the past and worry
about the future. Our curiosity is dulled by our daily routine, and
our fixation with technology and other distractions leaves little
room for attending to what might help or nurture us.

True, we may occasionally be captivated by a sunset or a work
of art. We may truly cherish our time with loved ones. But for the

most part, many of us live as if we have blinders on. We barely notice what's right in front of us, and our inborn sense of wonder seems to fade with the passing years.

All of this has consequences for the way we live our life. When we view the world through the narrow lens of unawareness, we don't see opportunities for growth or notice small gifts of beauty in everyday things. Resigned to an unsatisfying job, we automatically dismiss an entrepreneurial idea that might have real potential. Stuck in yet another traffic jam, we ignore the wild beauty of a flock of geese overhead.

Instead of exploring possibilities or appreciating the world around us, we slog along in our habitual way—and run up against the same old roadblocks. Unable to see a different path, we end up making the same decisions, no matter how unrewarding or self-defeating they may be. Changing that pattern begins with the conscious intent to see our self and the world through a more open lens.

The American philosopher Henry David Thoreau famously wrote about the path of mindfulness in his 1854 book, *Walden*. For two years, two months, and two days, he lived in a cabin in the woods of Massachusetts with the stated intent of becoming fully awake to his own life:

> I went to the woods because I wished to live deliberately, to front only the essential facts of life, and see if I could not learn what it had to teach, and not, when I came to die, discover that I had not lived.

His words remind us of the importance of intention. When we intend to "live deliberately"—that is, to live with awareness—we expand our understanding of who we are and strengthen our connection to the world around us.

> PRACTICE: **Notice where you are.** Try stepping out of your normal routine to really notice your home or neighborhood—almost as if you were seeing it for the first time. Don't judge or label what you discover. Simply observe with the sole intent of seeing, hearing, smelling, or touching what is actually there. *What surprises you about your environment as you pay closer attention?*

Less Impulse, More Intention

"The last time I made an impulse purchase, I maxed out my one remaining credit card," a friend once told me. "I was way over my head in debt, and I'd kept this one card only for emergencies. I didn't even carry it around with me because I didn't want to use it. Then one day I was bored and started browsing online. I saw this gorgeous pair of boots and a fantastic coat, and before I knew it, I'd blown fifteen hundred bucks."

Another friend described being taken to court by an ex-girl-friend after he posted some revealing photos of her online. "She'd been saying some nasty things about me, and I wanted to get back at her," he explained. "If I'd taken the time to think about it, I wouldn't have done it. The whole episode turned into a major headache and cost me a lot of money."

As people in recovery, most of us have experienced the negative fallout of an impulsive act. Impulse can lead us to pick a fight, walk out on a job, squander our paycheck, eat a half gallon of ice cream, or buy one drink that becomes the first of many. When we act impulsively, we don't take the time to think about potential consequences. We just do it, as the saying goes, and face the music (and regrets) later. But when we act with intention, we pause to consider the costs of an impulse *before* we act.

Impulsive actions are often triggered by distressing emotions such as anger, boredom, sorrow, or loneliness. Although our actions can feel instantaneous, there's almost always a moment—sometimes a mere split second—between the trigger and our response.

If we act impulsively, we can end up doing things that get us into trouble. If, on the other hand, we try to be more mindful of our intention, we can act in ways that produce a better outcome. Finding that space between the trigger and the action allows us to ask ourselves what kind of result we intend to achieve, giving us a precious chance to choose a wiser course.

> **REFLECTION:** "Intention is one of the most powerful forces there is. What you mean when you do a thing will always determine the outcome," wrote author Brenna Yovanoff. *Can you remember a time when acting on impulse got you into trouble? How could thinking about your intention beforehand have helped you make a different choice?*

The Power of Non-Doing

It takes a lot of effort to do nothing.

I'm not talking about the sitting-around-the-house, don't-get-off-the-couch kind of days in which we while away the hours by watching TV, scrolling through social media, or playing video games. I'm talking about consciously devoting a certain amount of time—say, five or ten minutes—to simply *being* instead of doing.

Our whole way of thinking goes against it. From childhood we're taught the importance of being productive. And if we can't be productive, we can at least be busy. The need to occupy our time with *something*—even mindless diversions—is deeply ingrained. Yet most of the world's great philosophers have noted the value of stepping away from the busyness of the world and devoting some time each day to simply being still.

Many years ago on a trip to England I entered one of the small, ancient churches that dot the countryside. The narrow stone building had a high vaulted ceiling and thick walls set with small leaded windows. On the altar were two stone coffins topped with carved effigies of a medieval lord and lady. Alone in the dim chapel, I sat for a long time on one of the plain wooden pews. The silence was profound, at once calm and deeply moving. I found myself transported through the centuries, at one with countless generations of worshipers who had come and gone before me. When I rose to leave, I passed a large rectangular table made of heavy, dark wood. It held a stack of white cards bearing the following inscription:

> Let thy soul walk softly in thee as a saint
> in heaven unshod,
>
> For to be alone with silence is to be alone with god.

I purchased one of the cards and framed it when I got home. To this day, when I take the time to read it, I feel again the calming stillness of that ancient church.

✳

We all need a quiet place within—a place where we can settle our mind and connect with our deeper self. It is from a place of inner stillness that the seeds of awareness, compassion, and contentment grow.

Yet the search for inner stillness is no small task for anyone. The world intrudes upon our thoughts, and the demands and distractions of daily life leave little time (or inclination) for self-reflection. For those of us in recovery, finding quietude can be especially challenging. After all, racing thoughts, persistent anxieties, and churning emotions were both a cause and a consequence of our compulsive behaviors. Even in recovery, it can be hard to feel at peace.

Meditation is one way to subdue the mental chatter and create a private sanctuary of inner calm. For thousands of years, human beings have practiced meditation as a path to spiritual growth. It is integral to ancient Hindu and Buddhist traditions, and most of the world's other major religions have adopted it in some form.

But meditation also has other benefits. Studies have shown that regular meditation can actually alter brain function and structure in ways that promote mental and physical health. One study concluded that mindfulness meditation programs reduce anxiety, depression, and pain about as effectively as antidepressant drugs, without the potential side effects.

Neuroscientist Richard Davidson, who studies the effects of meditation on the brain, believes that meditation doesn't only relieve stress. He says it can also increase happiness. "Most people still don't think of qualities like happiness as being a skill," he said in a 2012 interview. "It's typically conceptualized as a fixed trait." But, he pointed out, the brain is the *only* organ that is designed to change its very structure in response to experience and training. We have the power to enhance our own happiness because our brain is "wittingly or unwittingly being continuously shaped."

Addiction and all the crazy behaviors that went with it shaped our brain in ways that were detrimental to our well-being. We repeatedly practiced denial and deception, fed our compulsions, and internalized distorted beliefs about our self and others. Without realizing it, we changed our brain in ways that led to deepening unhappiness.

In recovery, we begin to undo the damage, replacing harmful habits with healthy choices. But making lasting, deep-rooted changes to our brain function takes time, effort, and consistent practice—just as toning our body does. Meditation is a practical tool that can help us to wittingly—that is, *intentionally*—change our brain in positive ways. At its core, meditation is essentially brain training. By learning to focus our attention on the here and now, we begin to connect with that quiet space from which true healing grows.

REFLECTION: "Meditation is not a way of making your mind quiet. It is a way of entering into the quiet that is already there—buried under the 50,000 thoughts the average person thinks every day," says author Deepak Chopra. *Where is your inner quiet?*

Just Breathe

You don't have to be a yogi, Buddhist, or New Age guru to practice meditation. In fact, you don't have to be anything at all other than a person who wants to enhance the overall quality of your life.

The word *meditation* might evoke an image of someone sitting cross-legged on the floor, eyes closed, oblivious to the world, but there are actually many ways to practice. We can meditate while sitting, standing, walking, or lying down, while practicing yoga or tai chi, and even while going about our tasks of daily life. We'll explore a few of these options later on, but a good way to begin is with following the breath—this is known as "breathing meditation."

To get started, find a place where you can sit comfortably and undisturbed for a few minutes. You can sit on a chair or on the floor with your legs crossed—whatever works for you. Straighten your spine without straining. Open your chest (your heart) as you hold your head erect. Rest your hands comfortably on your thighs, palms up, or clasp them gently in your lap.

Once you are comfortable, close your eyes. Take a moment to notice whatever is happening—sounds, smells, physical sensations, thoughts, and feelings. Be aware of the moment, without trying to do anything about it.

When you are ready, bring your attention to your breath. Notice how your breath feels as it moves through your nose and into your body. Notice how it feels as it leaves your body and returns to the air. It may help your concentration to focus on breathing in through your nose and out through your mouth. Or simply breathe normally.

Thoughts and emotions will enter your head. When they do, don't judge or evaluate them. Simply notice that you have thought or felt this particular thing. Then gently bring your attention back to your breath again and again as your thoughts, feelings, and sensations come and go in the background. Don't try to change anything. Just breathe.

When you are ready to come out of your meditation practice (don't worry about a "right" amount of time), open your eyes. Take a moment to notice your thoughts, feelings, and bodily sensations before you resume the rest of your day.

> **PRACTICE: Breathing break.** Try taking a "breathing break" now and then throughout the day. Simply breathe in through your nose and out through your mouth for five cycles. *Did you notice how you immediately feel calmer and more awake?*

Mindfulness and the Twelve Steps

The Twelve Steps were introduced to the world in 1939 with the publication of *Alcoholics Anonymous.* This groundbreaking book outlines a framework for recovery from alcoholism as experienced by AA founders Bill Wilson and Dr. Robert Smith and their recovery fellowship. The "Big Book," as it is widely known, presents two key ideas: first, that addiction is a disease and not, as was popularly believed, a character flaw or moral failing; and second, that recovery can be achieved primarily through the alcoholic's willingness to follow the Twelve Steps.

The AA approach to recovery proved so successful that today, Twelve Step programs can be found around the world, tackling everything from substance and behavioral addictions to emotional and mental health issues. And while the Steps have certainly drawn some criticism over the years, they continue to be the backbone of many addiction treatment programs and to guide millions of people in recovery from all kinds of compulsive behaviors.

The Twelve Steps of Alcoholics Anonymous

1. We admitted we were powerless over alcohol—that our lives had become unmanageable.

2. Came to believe that a Power greater than ourselves could restore us to sanity.

3. Made a decision to turn our will and our lives over to the care of God *as we understood Him.*

4. Made a searching and fearless moral inventory of ourselves.

5. Admitted to God, to ourselves, and to another human being the exact nature of our wrongs.

6. Were entirely ready to have God remove all these defects of character.

7. Humbly asked Him to remove our shortcomings.

8. Made a list of all persons we had harmed, and became willing to make amends to them all.

9. Made direct amends to such people wherever possible, except when to do so would injure them or others.

10. Continued to take personal inventory and when we were wrong promptly admitted it.

11. Sought through prayer and meditation to improve our conscious contact with God *as we understood Him,* praying only for knowledge of His will for us and the power to carry that out.

12. Having had a spiritual awakening as the result of these steps, we tried to carry this message to alcoholics, and to practice these principles in all our affairs.

For those of us in recovery, the Twelve Steps have endured, at least in part, because they support the almost universal human desire for purpose and meaning. In this respect, they have much in common with the practice of mindfulness.

Mindfulness is not simply an exercise in being awake. It is ultimately a path to personal growth, helping us learn how to live in harmony with our deepest values and with the world around us. Like the Twelve Steps themselves, mindfulness nurtures our innate potential to conduct our life with openness, honesty, and integrity.

That said, there are important differences between mindfulness and the Twelve Steps. For one thing, the Steps present a fixed set of guidelines for achieving self-improvement, while mindfulness assumes that we are our own best teacher—that by cultivating uncritical awareness of our thoughts and feelings, we begin to discover our own inner truths.

The Twelve Steps also prescribe reliance on a higher power, which—despite references in Steps Three and Eleven to "God *as we understood Him*"—can be an obstacle for people who reject the notion of such a being. Mindfulness, on the other hand, offers a more fluid concept of spirituality, one that springs from our own expanding awareness of our connectedness to the universal.

Finally, the Steps promote ethical living by placing a heavy emphasis on "defects of character," encouraging us to be vigilant in detecting and rectifying personal flaws. Mindfulness also promotes ethical living, but it does so within a framework of compassionate acceptance. Its underlying principle is that right actions emerge as awareness and understanding grow.

The differences between mindfulness and the Twelve Steps

reflect the different spiritual traditions from which they emerged. Mindfulness is central to Eastern traditions—such as Buddhism—which envision the holy as a quality that is inherent in each of us. The Twelve Steps grew out of Western traditions—specifically, Christianity—which view the holy as "transcendent, beyond, and other," according to author Diane Morgan:

> Western religion conceives the ultimate as God, and the goal of most people practicing the Western tradition is to know God, obey God, and form a loving and vital relationship with God. God is a person. Eastern thought tends to be nontheistic. It sees the ultimate as something transpersonal, and the goals of its practitioners are awareness and unity . . . So it might be accurate to say that while in Western thought the divine is a person, in Eastern thought, every person is ultimately divine.

Moreover, while mindfulness springs from Eastern spiritual tradition, the Twelve Steps reflect a specific branch of Western spiritual thought: Christian evangelism.

Before cofounding AA, Bill Wilson sought relief from alcoholism by joining a Christian fellowship called the Oxford Group. Founded in 1921 by a Lutheran minister who had had a conversion experience, the group was a loosely knit network of people who had surrendered to divine will and sought God's guidance in their daily life. By combining religious beliefs with social activities, they offered mutual support and tried to carry their message to others.

Among the Oxford Group's core principles were the beliefs that all people are sinners, that people can change, that confession is a prerequisite of change, and that changed people have an obligation to help others. Although Wilson eventually left the group, he later acknowledged its influence, writing in 1955: "The early A.A. got its ideas of self-examination, acknowledgment of character defects, restitution for harm done, and working with others straight from the Oxford Group."

The influence of the Oxford Group is evident throughout the Twelve Steps, which aim to guide us to a life of sobriety, honesty, integrity, and purpose. And as is true of the practice of mindfulness, the Steps encourage us to live more honorably through conscious commitment to self-reflection, humility, and concern for others. But mindfulness adds an important element to the quest for personal growth.

Mindfulness doesn't deny or sugarcoat the existence of human error. Rather, it guides us toward a more compassionate, more expansive kind of self-knowledge through the practice of awareness, nonjudgment, and kindness toward self and others. In essence, mindfulness helps us to find and nurture our own inner light.

REFLECTION: "In Asian languages, the word for 'mind' and the word for 'heart' are same," according to mindfulness guru Jon Kabat-Zinn. "So if you're not hearing mindfulness in some deep way as heartfulness, you're not really understanding it. Compassion and kindness towards oneself are intrinsically woven into it. You could think of mindfulness as wise and affectionate attention." *How can you practice compassion toward yourself today?*

From Powerlessness to Mindfulness

"We admitted we were powerless over alcohol—that our lives had become unmanageable."

The First Step is a big one. Whether we found recovery through Twelve Step programs or on another path, most of us had to confront the reality that we could not simply *will* our way to sobriety. We needed to radically shift our way of thinking. That meant letting go of the denial, self-deception, bravado, and hollow promises that had paved our self-destructive path: "I don't have a problem." "Things aren't that bad." "I can quit whenever I want." "I'll stop tomorrow."

It also meant accepting the fact that when it came to our compulsions, we had lost the power of choice. When we're addicted, our conscious will is lost to persistent, urgent need. We act automatically, without any thought or purpose beyond immediate gratification. We're like a puppet on a string, pulled this way and that by relentless cycles of highs and lows.

Yet addiction prevents us from seeing the truth of our situation. We cling stubbornly to our illusion of self-control. *I can manage my life perfectly well,* we tell ourselves, and we resist anyone's efforts to intervene. Only in brief moments of clarity do we see how out-of-control our life has become—how little power over addiction we actually have. Paradoxically, it's the recognition of our own powerlessness that allows us to break through the illusion of control and begin to develop our true inner power.

The road to recovery begins when we are willing to see what actually *is.* That is also the essence of mindfulness.

The value of seeing reality hit home for me one day when a

woman who runs a popular restaurant in a nearby community revealed how practicing mindfulness changed her life. She explained that she'd left the small town she grew up in to become an executive in a big-city advertising agency. But fulfilling her dream didn't make her happy. "I kept telling myself that this was what I'd always wanted, but I was binge drinking, popping pills, and my blood pressure was through the roof," she said.

Her doctor recommended mindfulness meditation, which she thought was "a waste of time," she admitted. "But I gave it a try, and lo and behold, I began to realize that my job was making me miserable. I discovered that what I really wanted was to move back home and open a farm-to-table restaurant." She grinned. "That was six years ago. It's a ton of work, but I've never been happier." By seeing and accepting the truth about her "dream job," she was able to find a more satisfying career path.

When we practice mindfulness (and it is *always* a practice, since we never achieve it perfectly or consistently), we start by paying attention to the reality of the present moment. And from our willingness to see things as they are, we begin to let go of the delusions, distractions, and misperceptions that keep us stuck. We learn to recognize our innate talents, deepest values, capacity for love, and inherent worth.

And as the light of self-awareness grows, so, too, does our power to fulfill the promise within us. In the words of the poet T. S. Eliot: "We shall not cease from exploration, and the end of all our exploring will be to arrive where we started and know the place for the first time."

PRACTICE: Feel the pause. In this variation of the seated breath awareness meditation, we develop our powers of concentration by paying attention to the natural pauses within each breathing cycle. Begin by sitting or lying in a comfortable position. Close your eyes. Take a moment to notice whatever is happening—sounds, smells, physical sensations, thoughts, and feelings. Be aware of the moment, but don't try to do anything about it. Breathe normally.

When you are ready, bring your attention to your breath. As your breath enters and exits your body, notice the tiny pause before each inhalation and exhalation. Don't try to force or emphasize the pause. Simply notice the stillness within it. Feel how that stillness is part of you, even in the midst of activity.

Distracting thoughts will enter your head. When they do, acknowledge them without judgment. Let them go and bring your attention back to the small, still pause before you inhale and exhale. When you are ready to come out of your meditation, open your eyes. *How can you connect with the stillness within you as you go about your day?*

●

Waking Up

When I heard the learn'd astronomer,

When the proofs, the figures, were ranged in columns
    before me,

When I was shown the charts and diagrams, to add,
    divide, and measure them,

When I sitting heard the astronomer where he lectured
    with much applause in the lecture-room,

How soon unaccountable I became tired and sick,

Till rising and gliding out I wander'd off by myself,

In the mystical moist night-air, and from time to time,

Look'd up in perfect silence at the stars.

—Walt Whitman, "When I Heard the Learn'd Astronomer"

AWARENESS IS FUNDAMENTAL to the practice of mindfulness. But what exactly does it mean to "bring your awareness" to something?

When I first tried practicing mindfulness, I had an idea that it meant I should think really hard about the object of my attention. I'd go into analytical mode and try to take in every last detail of my chosen target, noting the color, shape, size, texture—whatever quality seemed ripe for analysis. Needless to say, I didn't find my efforts particularly rewarding.

It took a while for me to figure out that awareness is a bit trickier than that. Yes, it involves paying attention, but it means doing so in an intuitive, "nonthinking" kind of way. In fact, I began to see that thinking can actually get in the way of awareness.

To understand how this works, consider my former mothering style, which was rooted in my own childhood. As a child, I was relentlessly bullied for being ugly, dirty, awkward, and poor. I learned to mask the pain, but years later I unknowingly carried it into my approach to child-rearing. I didn't want my kids to become the target of bullies, so I spent a lot of time looking for flaws before they ventured out into the world.

Understandably, my kids interpreted this hypervigilance as criticism. To this day, I regret that my overly analytical thoughts got in the way of clearly seeing them as they actually were—beautiful children in need of unconditional love and approval.

A friend once told me something similar after a high school concert we attended together. The students had performed beautifully, and I was deeply moved by the music. But my friend, whose daughter was a violinist, said that he had barely heard a single song. "I kept thinking that I didn't want her to mess up," he confessed, "so I was mostly focused on how she was doing." Unfortunately, his anxious thoughts prevented him from actually hearing the performance.

His experience is not uncommon. Whenever our thoughts take center stage, we risk not seeing reality because of the distracting ideas and distorting preconceptions that fill our head.

Thoughts and Awareness: What's the Difference?

Awareness starts with paying attention. But our attention is usually filtered through our thoughts—conscious or otherwise. Research suggests that we have between fifty thousand and seventy thousand thoughts each day, roughly the equivalent of forty-eight a minute. Some thoughts are focused, as when we're studying a map or following a complicated recipe or using a precision tool. Some are fleeting, like thoughts about the weather or someone's appearance or the latest news headlines. And some are buried so deep in our subconscious that we hardly recognize them as thoughts.

Regardless of their nature, thoughts of every kind can prevent us from being fully aware. That's because we tend to project our own beliefs, attitudes, and preconceptions onto everything we encounter. It's hard for us to see or experience much of anything without framing it within the context of our personal experiences. There's a simple explanation for this.

The human brain is built to see patterns. We automatically fill in missing information with what we expect to see and interpret current data based on past experience. That's how we learn, by building on prior knowledge. The ability to observe, interpret, and predict patterns has led to most of the advances that have improved human life. But as valuable as these skills are, they're not infallible. Sometimes, we see patterns where none exist, or we misinterpret data and reach the wrong conclusions. At other times, we distort reality to conform to our expectations.

This means that unless we make a conscious effort to become aware of the thoughts that shape our awareness, we may see things only as we *think* they are instead of as they actually are. As the British biologist Thomas Huxley once advised: "Sit down before fact as a little child, be prepared to give up every preconceived notion . . . or you shall learn nothing. I have only begun to learn content and peace of mind since I have resolved at all risks to do this."

Giving up our preconceived notions allows us to be open to new ideas and experiences that can expand knowledge and deepen understanding. But to give them up, we must first become aware of them. That's why mindfulness teaches us not only to pay attention to the world around us, but to pay attention to our thoughts. Most of us tend to give our thoughts the weight of reality when they are, in fact, just thoughts. With practice, we can learn to let go of erroneous preconceptions and self-defeating patterns of thinking that stand in the way of learning "content and peace of mind."

PRACTICE: **Letting go of thoughts.** This meditation is adapted from one developed by Insight Meditation Center cofounder Sharon Salzberg.

Begin by sitting or lying down comfortably. Close your eyes and take a moment to settle yourself. Breathe normally. When you are ready, bring your attention to your breath. Notice how it feels as it moves through your nose and into your body. Notice how it feels as it leaves your body and returns to the air. Gently say "breath" to yourself at the beginning of each inhalation and exhalation. When your mind wanders, recognize the intrusive thought as "not breath." Without judgment, let the thought go and bring your attention back to your breath. Continue in this manner until you are ready to come out of your meditation. *Can you let your thoughts fly away like birds on the wing?*

Shedding Light on Our Preconceptions

A story is told of a professor who went to a Zen master and asked him to explain the meaning of Zen. The master quietly poured a cup of tea. When the cup was full, he continued to pour, and the tea overflowed in a growing puddle. "Stop!" blurted the professor. "Why do you keep pouring when the cup is full?"

"I want to point out to you," the master said, "that you are similarly attempting to understand Zen while your mind is full. First, empty your mind of preconceptions before you attempt to understand Zen."

From our earliest infancy, our ideas about the world are formed by our experiences and immediate environment. If we are surrounded by love and security, we learn that the world is a welcoming place. If we experience rejection or trauma, we learn that the world is dangerous or even hostile. Between these two extremes, we pick up all kinds of lessons about what is good or bad, acceptable or unacceptable, normal or abnormal, safe or risky, attractive or unattractive, and valuable or worthless.

By the time we reach adulthood, the lessons we've learned have hardened into firm beliefs—preconceptions—that take on the weight of absolute truth. Rarely do we stop to question our beliefs or even to recognize that there might be alternative ways of looking at things. For example, if we've learned to place a high value on saving money, we may be critical of someone who spends "frivolously" on vacations—not taking into account that the other person may value experiences over savings. If we've been taught that children should always obey, we may fault parents whose rules are more relaxed than our own, not recognizing that they may value independence over compliance.

Preconceptions not only shape our opinions and beliefs. They can stop us from doing things like going on a date ("It'll just be a waste of time"), trying a new hobby ("It's probably too complicated"), making friends with someone of a different racial or cultural background ("We won't have anything in common"), or pursuing a promising job opportunity ("They won't hire me anyway"). They can prevent us from finding new solutions to problems and keep us stuck in a rut of defeatist thinking.

Most importantly, preconceptions can distort the way we see our self and others.

A few years ago, I attended a reception at an art museum in a nearby city. The event was a little out of my comfort zone—I anticipated that the other guests would be more "artsy" and knowledgeable than I am—but I wanted to see the exhibit and looked forward to meeting an old friend there. She didn't show up.

It turned out that her ex-husband—a doctor—had been arrested for driving while under the influence of narcotics. The local paper had published an article about the incident that included a picture of her and her husband at a charity event a few years earlier. "I got cold feet," she later apologized. "I started thinking that everyone would know about it, and they'd all be talking about me. I just couldn't face it."

I could understand her embarrassment. Still, it was her pre-conceptions—not actual reality—that led her to stand me up. She had convinced herself that she would be the center of attention without even considering the possibility that others might not know or care about the incident, or that those who did might feel compassion.

It's possible, of course, that had she gone, she might have encountered some negativity and ended up getting hurt. It's hard to know whether those hurt feelings would have been worse than what she was already experiencing thanks to her preconceptions. And that's the problem. When we accept our preconceptions as fact without testing their validity, we live in a world that is limited by our own way of looking at things. Sometimes we may be right. But we can just as easily be wrong and miss out on opportunities to learn, grow, and enjoy ourselves.

"We do not see things as they are, we see them as we are," observed the writer Anaïs Nin. In other words, when we view the world through the lens of our beliefs and expectations, we distort reality to conform to them. This can lead to all sorts of misunderstandings and missed opportunities.

The trick is to recognize our preconceptions and then to ask ourselves if they're built on false or incomplete information. When we learn to challenge our preconceptions, we open our heart and mind to new ideas and experiences that can lead to a fuller, more satisfying life.

REFLECTION: "Are you sure?" is a simple but powerful question posed by Zen master Thich Nhat Hanh to bring awareness to our preconceptions. Try writing this question on a piece of paper and placing it where you'll see it often. Remind yourself that faulty preconceptions can lead to faulty thinking and poor decisions. *What preconceptions can you recognize in yourself?*

Adjusting Your Default Setting: Avoiding Five Mental Traps

What are your habitual patterns of thinking? We all have them—those familiar thought patterns that spring up automatically in certain situations. They're so predictable that we tend to accept them as a defining aspect of ourselves: I'm someone who can't handle stress; I always freak out when things don't go right; I just naturally see the glass as half-empty; I will never be happy.

Our thinking habits run so deep that they can seem as natural as breathing, as if we were born with them. But in fact they are learned responses—like any other habit—established through repetition over long periods of time. True, our temperament may tend toward optimism or pessimism, equanimity or anxiety, extroversion or introversion. Anyone who has observed young children knows that personality traits emerge at a very young age. It's likely that we're naturally prone to certain types of thinking over others.

Still, our habits of thought are not part of our DNA. They haven't been with us from birth. Instead, they're acquired through a conditioning process in which our brain responds to particular stimuli in particular ways.

Think of a child who is frightened by her parents' constant

fighting and then feels traumatized by their divorce. Because she has no control over the situation, she comes to believe that she has no power to make anything better. Until she learns otherwise, this belief will shape her future responses to stress. Whether she's facing a bully at school, dealing with an abusive co-worker, or coping with conflict in an important relationship, her fear will trigger the deep-seated conviction that there is nothing she can do to improve things. Each repetition of this response reinforces her belief in her own helplessness.

By the time we reach adulthood, our brain contains a set of recognizable thought patterns that fire off automatically in response to certain people, places, and events—in a sense, our personal mental default setting. These are the ideas we tune in to again and again like a radio stuck on one station, as if there are no alternatives available to us.

Habitual thought patterns are great if they promote happiness, strength, and resilience. But as people in recovery, most of us grapple with thought patterns that simply don't work in our own best interest. Instead, they're mental traps that keep us stuck in self-defeating beliefs and behaviors. Let's look at five of the most damaging—and most common—mental traps.

Toxic Self-Criticism

Thoughtful self-reflection is a valuable way to identify and change personal behaviors that work against us. But toxic self-criticism is far from thoughtful. It's the kind of cruel, unthinking self-talk that deprives us of happiness and wounds our soul: "I'm fat." "I'm a loser." "I'm stupid." "I'm worthless." When toxic self-messages become habitual, we become our own worst enemy. Instead of empowering us to make things better, they lead to anxiety, depression, and hopelessness, crippling our ability to make constructive changes.

Catastrophic Thinking

With little or no evidence to support our conclusions, we assume that the worst has happened, or is about to. "Oh my god! My daughter isn't answering her phone. Maybe she was mugged or in an accident." "Oh, no! I lost my job. I'll never find another one and I'll end up homeless." "This weird pain in my head must mean I have brain cancer." The thing about catastrophic thinking is that, even though the disaster exists only in our head, our body responds as if it were real. We feel all the symptoms of stress—fear, agitation, racing thoughts, confusion—sapping the pleasure out of our day and making it harder to cope with whatever problems actually do arise.

All-or-Nothing Thinking

There's no middle ground in this type of thinking. Everything is either black or white, good or bad: "She's a terrible person!" "I've found the perfect job!" "Dinner was a total disaster!" "He's my Prince Charming!" Thoughts like these leave no room for shades of gray—yet few things in life are completely one thing or another. When we think in extremes, we become mentally rigid, judging our self and others harshly and building unrealistic expectations that inevitably disappoint us. Trapped in narrow corridors of perception, we can't detect and act on the countless nuances that color our daily interactions.

Overgeneralization

With this thought habit, we tend to see a single negative event (or even a series of them) as a permanent state of affairs. "Always," "never," "every," and "none" are some of the signposts of overgeneralization: "I'll always be a failure." "I'll never get that promotion." "None of my dreams will ever come true." "Every person in this family looks down on me." In reality, life is rarely that consistent or absolute. We all struggle. We all go through ups and downs. When we project negative consequences far into the future, we're assuming that nothing will change. We forget that we ourselves have the capacity to change in ways that can yield more positive outcomes.

Confirmation Bias

In this type of thinking, we see only what we expect to see and ignore the rest. A well-known study at Brigham and Women's Hospital in Boston dramatically illustrated this phenomenon. Researchers asked twenty-four radiologists to examine five scans of patients' lungs to search for cancerous nodules. Each scan showed an average of ten nodules. The last one included an image of a gorilla, *forty-eight times larger than the nodules.* Despite its obvious presence, 83 percent of the radiologists did not report seeing the gorilla. The radiologists missed the gorillas because, as they said, *"What we become focused on becomes the center of our world, and it shapes what we can and cannot see."* This principle plays out in our daily life when we see only the things that support our opinions and dismiss or ignore contradictory evidence. As a result, our thoughts run on a closed loop that limits our knowledge and prevents us from considering other, possibly more accurate ways of understanding our world.

✳

These habitual patterns of faulty thinking have an enormous impact on our quality of life. They can cause us to give up in the face of obstacles, prevent us from working through difficulties, and keep us stuck in unhealthy patterns of relating to others. After all, our actions are the physical expression of our thoughts. Yet, like most habits, thought patterns usually operate so far beneath our consciousness that we're barely aware of them. How, then, can we begin to change them?

As a first step, we can bring them out of the shadows and recognize them for what they are: thinking habits that have become automatic through constant repetition. Then, we can work to change those habits with the same dedication that we apply to other aspects of our recovery.

There's no doubt that changing our thought patterns can be challenging. We may even believe that our thoughts are beyond our control. That is not the case. As the writer Marianne Williamson explains: "You may believe that you are responsible for what you do, but not for what you think. The truth is that you are responsible for what you think, because it is only at this level that you can exercise choice. What you do comes from what you think."

One of the primary benefits of mindfulness practice is learning to recognize our thoughts as thoughts. They are not reality unless we make them so. As we become aware of our self-defeating thought patterns—those mental default settings that hold us back—we can remind ourselves again and again that thoughts are simply thoughts. Then we can choose to let them go.

REFLECTION: "The world as we have created it is a product of our thinking," said Albert Einstein. "It cannot be changed without changing our thinking." *What habitual thought patterns can you recognize in yourself? Which ones will you choose to let go of—just for today?*

Seeing without Judging

Almost from the moment of birth, we humans judge every aspect of our world. It's a survival reflex that lets us instantly identify safety or danger, friend or foe.

Judgment is the guiding force behind most of our decisions, from whether we have eggs or cereal for breakfast to where we live and whom we marry. When we exercise poor judgment, we end up doing things that can get us into trouble, like rekindling an abusive relationship or drinking and driving. When we use good judgment, we do things that can promote our well-being, like reaching out to an old friend or getting into recovery. In a way, the quality of our life is a reflection of the judgments we've made, good and bad, big and small.

But what about *nonjudgment,* the mindful practice of observing without judging? What can we gain from that practice? Simply put, nonjudgment allows us to step back and see things more objectively. It also lays the groundwork for a more compassionate worldview.

A story is told of an Indian king who entered a city in which everyone was blind. The king rode in on a magnificent elephant and wanted to impress the people with his majesty. He ordered six men to feel the elephant and describe it to the city's inhabitants.

One man felt the legs and told the crowd that the elephant was like four pillars. The second man felt the tail and described it as a broom. Patting its side, the third man said it was like a wall. For the man at the ears, it was like a carpet; for the one at its trunk, like a pipe. At its tusks, the last man declared the elephant was like a pair of horns. Each had reached what seemed to be a reasonable conclusion—but their judgment was based on incomplete evidence.

The problem with making judgments is our tendency to slap labels on things before we fully understand them. When we decide that something is good or desirable without looking beyond our first impression, we can find ourselves signing contracts, taking on debt, accepting job offers, or investing in money-making schemes that we later come to regret.

Similarly, if we prematurely label something as bad or undesirable, we can deprive ourselves of a potential benefit—something I experienced firsthand. When I was young, I turned down a full scholarship to a good university because I thought its location was too "boring." I was not only wrong about the location. I lost out on a wonderful opportunity to improve my life. If I had practiced nonjudgment (something I'd never heard of at the time), I would have kept an open mind and gathered more information before making an evidence-based decision.

But the benefits of nonjudgment go far beyond helping us to become more awake and aware decision-makers. Nonjudgment opens the door to a more compassionate understanding of our self and others.

How many times a day do you judge other people? If you're like most of us, you probably do it a lot without realizing it: She looks haggard. He could stand to lose a little weight. She's too old to wear that skirt. He needs a haircut. If someone pulls into a parking space ahead of us, he's a moron or a jerk. If someone's using food stamps in the checkout line, she's lazy or a cheater. All these labels are based on snap judgments. All are made more or less automatically. And all diminish the quality of our life.

One of the most-quoted lines from the Bible is "Judge not, that ye be not judged." There's a lot of wisdom in that advice. Judging others sets up barriers between *us* and *them*. We tell ourselves that the people we judge are different from us—odd, arrogant, or unacceptable in some fundamental way. But when we define the entirety of who they are based on a single aspect of their appearance or behavior, we deny our common humanity, making our world a harsher, lonelier place.

This realization can strike us unexpectedly, perhaps especially when we are hurting. Years ago, when my marriage was falling apart and one of my children was struggling with addiction, I went through the motions of my daily routine, but I was always knotted up with worry and grief. One day while I was in a grocery store, hiding my pain behind my "public" face, I had a sort of epiphany. Looking at other shoppers, I was forcibly struck by the realization that nobody knows what burdens other people may be carrying. We all do our best to act "normally" in public. But who knows what private struggles our fellow beings are coping with?

One of my favorite reminders of this truth is found in a Nar-Anon Family Group booklet: "Remember all people are always changing. When we judge them, we judge on what we believe we know of them, failing to realize that there is much we do not know, and that they are constantly changing as they try for better or worse to cope with life."

Nonjudgment removes the blinders from our eyes, allowing us to see that life's struggles, disappointments, pain, and loss come to everyone. Whatever our differences, we honor our common humanity when we begin to replace judgment with compassion.

✳

Unfortunately, for many of us who have experienced any problematic compulsive behavior, the person we judge most harshly is our self. Even when we know that addictions and compulsions are illnesses much like other chronic conditions, they seem to go hand-in-hand with shame. Why?

For one thing, although attitudes are slowly changing, addiction and recovery still carry a stigma. Many people continue to view addiction as a sign of weakness or poor character despite decades of research that has shown it to be a complex disorder manifested by a broad set of behaviors, tendencies, and habits. Many of us have internalized the stigma, concluding that *we are weak and of poor character.* Moreover, a lot of us didn't like ourselves very much even before we became addicted. Poor self-image is often an important contributing factor in addiction. And then, during the course of our disordered living and thinking, many of us did things that we're ashamed of, further damaging our self-respect.

In recovery, we work to make amends for harm we have caused others. But we sometimes fail to make amends to our self. Instead, we tend to judge ourselves without mercy, inflicting layers of shame and guilt on our already-battered ego. We tell ourselves that because we have done something wrong, we must be a horrible person. Unfortunately, beating ourselves up—like picking at a wound—only weakens our ability to heal.

A man I met in a support group illustrated this truth when he described his long alienation from his children. "I had a raging drug problem for almost five years," he said. "I dropped out of my kids' lives. Even after I got clean, I didn't reach out to them because I didn't think I deserved them." It wasn't until his fourteen-year-old son contacted him that he began to rebuild his relationship with his kids.

"They're the most important thing in the world to me," he said with a catch in his voice. "But I don't know if I would've ever found the courage to reconnect on my own. I hated myself too much." For him, as for many of us, the pain of self-judgment kept the pain of addiction eternally fresh and raw.

Nonjudgment—the ability to observe and accept without labels—allows us to see ourselves in a clearer, kinder light. We acknowledge our mistakes and do our best to set things right. But we also recognize that we lacked the wisdom and skills that might have enabled us to make better choices. Our harmful actions sprang not from "badness" but from unawareness, something we are working hard to correct. When we stop viewing our self through the narrow lens of self-judgment, our perspective begins to expand. We come to see that like all human beings, we, too, are deserving of kindness and compassion—not judgment.

> **PRACTICE: Nonjudgment day.** Try going an entire day without judging anyone, including yourself. When judgmental thoughts arise, pause to examine them. Notice their content and how they make you feel. Notice how they affect your perception of the world. Then, with conscious intention, choose to let them go. *What can you do to observe more and judge less?*

Clarity through Humility

"If I have seen further it is by standing on the shoulders of giants," wrote Sir Isaac Newton, one of the world's greatest scientists, in 1675. Nearly three hundred years later, Albert Einstein made an equally humble remark in a letter to a friend: "People like you and I, though mortal of course like everyone else, do not grow old no matter how long we live . . . [We] never cease to stand like curious children before the great mystery into which we were born."

It may seem surprising that two men of such spectacular intellect held a lifelong attitude of humility. But in reality, humility was key to their success—for it was humility that allowed them to approach their work with an open and curious mind. That same humble attitude of openness and curiosity is required of us if we are to fully realize the vast potential of our own life.

I once heard a man in a Twelve Step meeting say that he never admits he is wrong and never backs down. "You have to stand up for yourself," he explained. He stopped coming to the meetings not long after that, but I sometimes wonder about him and how he is doing. If he's like a lot of us, it probably took him a while to sort out the vital role that humility plays in our personal growth.

Humility has nothing to do with being meek or submissive or thinking of ourselves as less than anybody else. It also has nothing to do with having high or low self-esteem. Simply put, humility is about letting go of the belief that we know all we need to know. When we practice humility, we learn to question our own certainties, to admit that we don't have all the answers, and to ask for help when we need it. We accept that we, like all people, have flaws and limitations. And because humility opens our heart and mind to new ways of seeing things, it allows us to learn from our mistakes. Paradoxically, humility is an expression of confidence in our own worth because we don't have to pretend to be perfect in order to feel worthwhile.

Humility is widely recognized as an important quality in effective leadership. An article in the *Harvard Business Review* titled "The Best Leaders Are Humble Leaders" noted that "without humility you are unable to learn." That's because when we think we know best, we close our mind to new, possibly better ideas. What's more, leaders who model the ability to admit mistakes, learn from criticism, and listen to others' point of view make it okay for subordinates to do the same, creating an environment of teamwork rather than one-upmanship.

The same qualities of humility that enhance leadership also improve personal relationships. I once overheard a woman say to a friend, "If my kid was acting that way, I know what *I'd* do"—the implication being that she knew how to handle the situation and her friend needed to hear it. The urge to tell others what to do may spring from an earnest desire to be of help. But we can never know for sure what is best for someone else. What we do know is that being able to listen with an open mind goes a long way toward promoting understanding and mutual respect.

Perhaps surprisingly, humility can also help to improve the relationship we have with our self.

It's easy to confuse humility with low self-esteem, something many of us in recovery struggle with. "I already think poorly of myself. I don't need to practice humility," you may be thinking. But an exaggerated sense of *low self-worth* is as much an obstacle to humility as an overblown sense of importance. For when we cling stubbornly to a negative self-image, we close our mind to other, more enlightened perspectives.

Humility opens our mind to the reality that mistakes and confusion are part of the human condition—for us and for everyone. It frees us from the harmful belief that we have to be "perfect" in order to be worthy of love and respect. And it allows us to value our self as we value others, not ranked in some merit-based hierarchy, but as equally flawed and vulnerable sojourners on this journey called life.

When we practice humility, we learn to drop our pretenses and explore the mystery of our own existence. As the writer Rainer Maria Rilke advised:

> Be patient toward all that is unsolved in your heart and try to love the questions themselves, like locked rooms and like books that are now written in a very foreign tongue . . . Live the questions now. Perhaps you will then gradually, without noticing it, live along some distant day into the answer.

PRACTICE: Stargazing. In the poem at the beginning of this chapter, Walt Whitman captures the difference between thinking and awareness when he leaves the lecture hall to look up "in perfect silence at the stars." Try this yourself.

Sit or stand comfortably outside or near a window through which you can see the night sky. Breathe normally. Take a moment to settle your thoughts. Then, pick an object in the sky—the moon or star or even a constellation. Observe it with your senses fully engaged for as long as you like. Don't analyze it. Don't try to figure it out. Simply listen to the silence, feel the texture of the distance, and see the clear, bright light that has come from so far away. *What does the mystery of the universe feel like to you?*

Enlightened Self-Awareness

The bud
stands for all things,
even for those things that don't flower,
for everything flowers, from within, of self-blessing;
though sometimes it is necessary
to reteach a thing its loveliness,
to put a hand on its brow
of the flower
and retell it in words and in touch
it is lovely
until it flowers again from within, of self-blessing;
as Saint Francis
put his hand on the creased forehead
of the sow, and told her in words and in touch
blessings of earth on the sow, and the sow

continued

began remembering all down her thick length,
from the earthen snout all the way
through the fodder and slops to the spiritual curl of the tail,
from the hard spininess spiked out from the spine
down through the great broken heart
to the sheer blue milken dreaminess spurting and shuddering
from the fourteen teats into the fourteen mouths sucking and
blowing beneath them:
the long, perfect loveliness of sow.

—Galway Kinnell, "St. Francis and the Sow"

I REMEMBER STANDING in the doorway one summer afternoon after another fractious conversation with my adult daughter. As she was about to storm off, I exclaimed in a burst of exasperation, "I just want you to have a happy life!"

She rolled her eyes. "Okay. I will." She was being sarcastic, but she made her point. It's not in our power to confer happiness on somebody else. Just as it's not in our power to confer happiness on ourselves.

Or is it? We all long for happiness. But is it possible to become happier simply by choosing to do so? Research suggests that it is.

What Is Happiness?

More than twenty-three hundred years ago, the Greek philosopher Aristotle asserted that happiness is the ultimate purpose of human existence. He wasn't talking about the pursuit of pleasure or the gratification of desires, although he wasn't opposed to either one. Instead, he described happiness as an enduring condition of physical and mental well-being that comes from living each day to the best of our ability—"an activity of the soul in accordance with virtue."

More recently, an entire branch of social science—positive psychology—has emerged to explore the meaning of happiness and how to get it. Building on Aristotle's observations, most practitioners of positive psychology describe happiness as a deep sense of well-being that persists despite life's inevitable struggles and disappointments.

To put it another way, those who study the subject don't define happiness as one of those feel-good moods we experience when something wonderful happens to us. Instead, they see it as an overall sense of contentment and satisfaction with our life. Moreover, they contend that personal happiness can be increased by developing certain skills—skills that can be learned by everyone. The psychologist Richard Davidson observed:

> I think that that's a very different conception of happiness, one that is more enduring and I think more genuine in the sense that it's a kind of happiness that is not dependent on external circumstances . . . if you think about [happiness] more as a skill, then it's something that can be enhanced through training.

Davidson and other researchers have found that the regular practices of mindfulness and meditation can promote the development of happiness skills—regardless of our individual psychological makeup.

Scientists have long noted that there seems to be a genetic basis for many personality traits, including depression and addiction. They have also concluded that genetics plays a role in how happy we are.

Estimates vary, but studies suggest that happiness is about 50 percent genetic. Some people are just born with a happier (or unhappier) disposition than others. Another 10 percent of happiness seems to come from our circumstances—job, home life, and so on. The remaining 40 percent stems from our attitudes, thoughts, and behaviors—factors that are well within our power to improve.

As the Buddha observed: "Happiness does not depend on what you have or who you are. It solely relies on what you think."

To understand how what we believe, think, or do can impact our happiness, consider the complex interplay of neurochemicals in our brain. Dopamine, serotonin, endorphins, and GABA—all targeted by addictive substances and behaviors—are linked to feelings of happiness, whether euphoric or serene. The highs and lows we experience through the course of addiction hinge on the changing levels of these and other neurochemicals in our natural reward system.

In recovery, one of our main challenges is to replace artificial stimulation with healthier, more life-affirming choices. Things like exercise, physical intimacy, and setting and achieving goals can trigger the release of "feel-good" chemicals. So can compassion, self-knowledge, virtue, and purpose. These are the qualities we build through the practice of mindfulness. When we do things that make us feel good about our self—developing our talents, living up to our values, nurturing our relationships, and contributing to our community—we are rewarded with positive feelings.

Martin Seligman, a pioneer of the positive psychology movement, asserts that lasting happiness is built on two pillars: engagement—devoting attention to work, relationships, and community—and meaning, which "consists of knowing what your highest strengths are, and using them to belong to and in the service of something larger than you are."

But before we can act in accordance with our interests, talents, and values, we must first discover what they are—in essence, who we are. That is the ultimate work of mindfulness.

Paying attention to the day-to-day moments of our life is about much more than simply expanding our awareness and letting go of self-defeating thoughts and behaviors. It's about learning to listen to our own inner voice, that kernel of *self* that is always there to guide us. As the Chinese philosopher Lao-Tzu wrote, "At the center of your being you have the answer; you know who you are and you know what you want."

As we acquire a deeper understanding of who we really are, we begin to build the skills that lead to a happier, more satisfying life.

> PRACTICE: **Favorite song.** Some songs can instantly make us feel happier. Choose a favorite song that does that for you, drop whatever else you're doing, and listen—really listen to the song. You can sit or stand, tap your feet, dance around the room, sing along out loud—whatever it takes for you to fully experience the joy of the music. When it's done, play it again, over and over for as long as you like. *Have you noticed how what we choose to put into our head can change the way we feel?*

Enlightened Self-Awareness

Jenny: Do you ever dream, Forrest, of who you wanna be?

Forrest: Who I'm gonna be? Aren't I gonna be me?

Jenny: You'll always be you. Just another kind of you. You know?

The lead character in the movie *Forrest Gump* was such an uncomplicated soul that he didn't grapple with questions about who he was. He was simply, unapologetically himself. For most of us, however, discovering a firm sense of personal identity is a long and often confusing process of trial and error.

As young children, our sense of self is largely defined by the way we're treated by our closest family members. In our teen years, we may try on different masks to see which ones feel right—I'm a rebel, or a nerd, or a party animal, or a jock. In early adulthood, we take on more substantive roles—employee, spouse, parent, volunteer. Through it all, we discover our likes and dislikes, strengths and weaknesses, beliefs and values.

But the process of self-discovery doesn't happen in a neutral environment. Our brain is hardwired to *interpret* experiences and circumstances, to impose meaning that directly impacts our understanding of who we are. Children, who naturally believe they are the center of the world, tend to think of themselves as the cause of everything that happens to them. If they are treated with warmth and encouragement, they conclude that they are worthy of love and acceptance. If they are treated with coldness and criticism, they come to believe that they are flawed and unworthy.

These early beliefs about our self—whether we're good or bad, worthy or unworthy—become the prism through which we filter subsequent experiences. That explains why, if we feel worthy, we're able to savor our successes and shrug off our failures. But if we feel unworthy, we minimize our successes and dwell on our failures. In either case, we try to fit what happens to us into our understanding of who we are.

Addiction imposes another layer onto our existing self-image. Whether we have high or low self-worth at the outset, addiction inflicts damage on our sense of self. When we're addicted, we behave in ways we're not proud of. We lead a life of secrets and deception. We distance ourselves from others. We neglect our interests and talents. We feed our compulsions. And our self-confidence is shaken when we discover that we've lost control of our own life.

In a very real sense, recovery—like mindfulness—is about undoing the damage that has been imposed on our sense of self. It involves getting past the clutter of harmful thoughts and false beliefs and discovering—maybe for the first time—who we really are.

As we undertake this work, it's important to examine our mistakes and character flaws. After all, taking responsibility for our actions is a critical step in personal growth. But we miss the big picture if we focus on our defects without also acknowledging our wounds, struggles, and virtues. Like the blind men examining the elephant, we get the wrong idea if we fail to see our self within the larger context of the experiences that helped shape us.

The French have a saying: *Tout comprendre c'est tout pardonner*—to understand all is to forgive all. This same principle of compassion applies to our quest for self-knowledge, for it is compassion that allows us to accept our own imperfections. Many of us have the mistaken belief that we can't be deserving of love or acceptance until we've removed all our flaws—or until we have suffered enough to atone for past mistakes. This line of thinking is like living with a perpetual cloud over the sun, for our ideal of human perfection is simply not attainable. Not for us. Not for anyone.

As we journey toward a deeper understanding of our self, the practice of mindfulness guides us toward a more enlightened form of self-awareness—that is, self-knowledge tempered by self-compassion. And as our understanding of who we are expands, we begin to accept the many parts of our self—the good, bad, and indifferent—and know in our heart that we are worthy of love and happiness just as we are.

To remind ourselves of this truth, it is helpful to remember these words from the Buddha: "You can search throughout the entire universe for someone who is more deserving of your love and affection than you are yourself, and that person is not to be found anywhere. You, yourself, as much as anybody in the entire universe, deserve your love and affection."

> REFLECTION: In the poem at the beginning of this chapter, Galway Kinnell celebrates "the long, perfect loveliness of sow." *What personal "imperfections" can you learn to accept as part of the "perfect loveliness" of you?*

A Fresh Take on a "Fearless Moral Inventory"

Seven of the Twelve Steps suggest identifying and correcting our character defects, beginning in Step Four with the words "Made a searching and fearless moral inventory of ourselves." In the six Steps that follow it, we're advised to admit our mistakes, to seek help from a higher power, to make amends wherever possible, and, in Step Ten, to be on the lookout for future errors: "Continued to take personal inventory and when we were wrong promptly admitted it."

Millions of people have been helped by Twelve Step programs, relying on their message of personal accountability to turn their lives around. These seven Steps in particular promote the kind of honest self-examination that cuts through denial and encourages us to confront reality. After all, as TV personality Dr. Phil says, "You can't change what you don't acknowledge."

But as useful as these Steps may be, they stop short of guiding us toward a more expansive understanding of who we are. They invite us to lay bare our flaws but shed little light on our other qualities. The emphasis on removing "defects of character" suggests that there is something inherently wrong within us that can be quelled only through constant vigilance.

The practice of mindfulness offers an alternative way of coping with our human imperfections.

Since the dawn of civilization, thinkers and spiritual leaders have explored the nature of good and evil. Ancient moral codes such as the Ten Commandments and the seven deadly sins attest to the widely recognized truth that we humans are far from perfect. More recently, scholars have explained the negative aspects of human nature in psychological terms.

The Swiss psychologist Carl Jung asserted that everyone has a "dark" side—damaging thoughts, feelings, and impulses that harm our self or others if we act on them. He called this the "shadow self." (I once heard a person in recovery call it the "beast inside me.") In the view of psychoanalyst Sigmund Freud, the human psyche has three parts: the id, ego, and superego. The id is the bundle of needs and impulses we're born with. If they're satisfied, we experience comfort, security, and pleasure. If denied, we feel pain, frustration, and anger. As we mature, the ego and superego emerge to help us manage our needs and impulses in socially appropriate, morally acceptable ways. But the id stays with us, a source of drive and energy, but also of greed, impulsiveness, and selfishness—a "dark, inaccessible part of our personality," in Freud's words.

However we define it, the dark side of human nature—those jealous, greedy, vengeful thoughts and impulses that crop up from seemingly out of nowhere—exists in all of us. Our challenge is not to become free of imperfections, which is impossible. It is to improve our skill at managing the potentially destructive parts of our nature.

In Buddhist tradition, our thoughts and actions aren't labeled "good" or "bad." Instead, they're labeled "skillful" or "unskillful." Simply put, skillful thoughts and actions are those that promote the well-being of our self and others. Unskillful thoughts and actions are those that harm our self and others.

Mindfulness builds on this tradition, teaching us to ask ourselves, "Will my thoughts and actions lead to satisfaction and happiness? Or will they cause trouble and unhappiness?" In other words, are they skillful or unskillful?

A group of fifth graders who took part in a mindfulness program at their school in Oakland, California, worked on becoming more skillful in their behavior. The results were impressive. One boy recalled, "[I] was losing at baseball and I was about to throw the bat," when his mindfulness training allowed him to control the impulse. A girl reported hearing less of "the gossip inside my head: I'm stupid, I'm fat, or I'm going to fail math." Another boy defined skillful thinking more succinctly: it's "not hitting someone in the mouth," he said.

These students learned a valuable lesson: that they didn't have to follow through on their potentially destructive impulses.

Instead, by bringing awareness to their thoughts *before* they acted, they were able to behave in nonharmful ways.

Many of us who have struggled with addiction have experienced deprivation or trauma, or we lacked positive guidance at critical moments in our life. Addiction further disrupted our maturation. As a result, we may not have acquired the skills we need to make wise choices. Instead, we sometimes fall into a cycle of repeating the same mistakes and then concluding that there's something terribly wrong with us.

When we practice mindfulness, we begin to see that the suffering we cause our self and others is not a matter of "defects of character." It's a lack of know-how.

A woman I met in a Twelve Step study group reminded me of this truth one day over coffee. She told me that she'd always longed for a lasting, stable relationship, but all her relationships had been the exact opposite—short and volatile. Until now. "I met someone I really like, and I didn't want to screw it up," she said. "So I started seeing a counselor. She pointed out that when something upsets me, I usually attack first and ask questions later. Which obviously doesn't work. So now, when I start to tense up, I focus on listening and trying to understand where my partner is coming from."

She smiled as the color rose in her face. "I have a partner. Imagine that!"

Although this woman didn't label her changed behavior as "skillful," a higher level of awareness allowed her to act in ways that improved her relationship with someone she cares deeply about. Similarly, as we become more self-aware and learn to think before we act, we get better at managing our unskillful impulses and behaving in ways that bring greater happiness.

> **REFLECTION:** "I did then what I knew how to do. Now that I know better, I do better," wrote the author Maya Angelou. Her words underscore our lifelong potential to become more skillful in how we deal with the world. *What skillful choices will you make today?*

The Stories We Tell Ourselves

One night when my younger daughter was about six years old, I was driving home through an intense rainstorm. The kids were quiet in the back seat, probably picking up on the anxiety I felt as we crept along through the murky darkness. Water streamed down the windshield. The steady thump of the inadequate wipers was the only sound inside the car.

Suddenly, my daughter's voice rang out. "I don't like this movie!" she wailed.

I was amused, the way adults are at the unpredictable pronouncements of children. But the comment has stayed with me through the years, probably because it contained an element of truth: We are all stars in a story (or movie) of our own making. And whether we're hero or villain, survivor or victim, the stories we tell ourselves become the narrative of our life.

Stories are the way we make sense of things that happen to us and the choices we make: Why did my parents get a divorce? Why did my mother abandon me? Why is my friend avoiding me? Why didn't I get a promotion? Why did I have that affair? Like fictional stories, our personal narrative contains struggles and adversity, heroes who help us and scoundrels who hurt us, and, of course, a compelling main character—our self—whose identity evolves with our changing perceptions.

When I was a teenager growing up in an oppressively unhappy home, I attributed many of my family's struggles to my belief that I was an obnoxious, unlovable kid. As a young adult, I shifted the blame for our misery onto my parents, casting them as uncaring villains and myself as a perpetual victim. I was well into middle age before I could see myself not as a victim but as a survivor whose parents, though hampered by their own unresolved issues, had done the best they could.

My perceptions changed not because I learned anything different about my childhood. The facts remained the same: my father was frequently abusive and tyrannical; my mother was depressed and defeated. But as time passed, I was able to tell myself a different story about my family. I saw how my parents' own childhoods—scarred by serious illness, extreme poverty, alcoholism, divorce, and suicide—were part of a larger, multigenerational story of struggle and survival. I saw how various parts of the story had affected other family members and how they had all tried, with varying degrees of success, to cope with trauma and hardship.

By changing my perspective and widening the lens through which I viewed my story, I learned to let go of blame. I began to understand myself—and my family—in a clearer, more compassionate light.

It's human nature to impose meaning on events. From the moment of birth, we try to understand and interpret our experiences. But when our interpretation is faulty or incomplete—when we draw the wrong conclusions from what has happened to us—

we can end up creating a distorted personal narrative that limits our ability to create a happier, more satisfying life. As the artist Rabih Alameddine wrote, "What happens is of little significance compared with the stories we tell ourselves about what happens. Events matter little, only stories of events affect us."

The stories we tell ourselves have a profound effect on our sense of who we are. According to professor Dan McAdams, who has spent years studying what he calls "narrative identity," there are two major types of personal narratives: stories of redemption and stories of contamination.

Redemptive stories are those in which people overcome hardship and in the process become stronger, wiser, and more empathetic. A core theme of their personal story is belief in their own worth and confidence in their ability to handle whatever happens to them.

A former neighbor of mine—a counselor who worked with troubled teens—seemed to embody the redemptive narrative. He was like a lot of the decent, conscientious fathers in our neighborhood. But unlike them, his background included gangs, substance abuse, and incarceration. "I was a rebellious, know-it-all kid," he once told me. "A tough guy. But when I was twenty-two, I ended up in the county house of corrections for the third time. There were guys in there forty, fifty, sixty years old. I figured that was going to be me if I didn't change."

He earned his GED in jail, and when he got out, he took classes at a community college. Eventually, he found a job working with "kids just like me," married his high school sweetheart, and started a family. How was he able to turn his life around?

"I always knew I could do something good with my life," he said. "Make a difference, you know? It just took me a while to figure out what it was." Although his early life was marred by unskillful choices, his belief that he could use his experiences for "something good"—his redemptive narrative identity—enabled him to create a more rewarding life story.

Contamination stories, on the other hand, are those in which people get trapped in their struggles. Unable to make any sense of their misery, they tell themselves that life has singled them out for suffering and there is nothing they can do to make things better.

One of my close relatives falls into this second category.

As a child, she was beautiful, outgoing, and full of fun. But a series of personal traumas—her parents' divorce, her father's rejection, the death of a boyfriend—seemed to drain all the liveliness from her. She developed eating disorders and, in her late twenties, moved in with a man who was reportedly abusive.

We talk on the phone occasionally, and the conversations usually go something like this: She hates her job, but "I'll probably never get anything better." Her boyfriend is mean, but "it's better than being alone." She's unhappy about her weight, but "my looks are gone, so it doesn't matter anyway." I try to be supportive, but she seems convinced—for now, anyway—that she was born to be a victim. This personal narrative, more than anything else, has kept her trapped in a life of grinding unhappiness.

The most important thing about narrative identities—whether of redemption or contamination—is that they tend to become self-fulfilling prophecies. That's because we unconsciously behave in ways that perpetuate the story we've created for ourselves. Like actors following a script, we adopt attitudes, repeat behaviors, and make choices that conform to our self-imposed storyline.

Mindfulness can be an important tool for changing the script. When we bring awareness to our thoughts, we begin to challenge long-held perceptions. We reality-check the meaning we've attached to our experiences. We reassess our view of events and gain a clearer perspective of our role in them. And freed from a damaging narrative identity, we can begin to write a more rewarding script for our story's lead character—our self.

> **PRACTICE: Get out of your rut.** Sometimes, taking a physical break from our usual routine can open our mind to new ways of seeing things. Try doing one new thing this week, such as taking a walk in an unfamiliar neighborhood, attending a meeting or worship service you've never been to, shopping in a different grocery store, or trying a new sport—even if it's shooting a few baskets in the local park. Practice nonjudgmental observation and keep your senses wide open. *How can new experiences open your mind to new ways of seeing yourself?*

What Shame, Guilt, and Anger Can Teach Us

"I never learned hate at home, or shame. I had to go to school for that," wrote the social activist Dick Gregory. In his essay "Shame," he described the humiliation he felt as a seven-year-old when his teacher ridiculed him in front of his classmates for being poor, on welfare, and fatherless:

> "We're collecting this money for you and your kind, Richard Gregory . . . And furthermore," she said, looking right at me, her nostrils getting big and her

lips getting thin and her eyes opening wide, "we
know you don't have a Daddy" . . .

I walked out of school that day and for a long time
I didn't go back very often.

There was shame there.

Now there was shame everywhere.

Gregory carried that shame with him for years, fueled by the
secret belief that he was unworthy of love or respect or kindness
or acceptance. Many of us in recovery have carried or continue
to carry a similar sense of shame. In fact, numerous studies have
shown a strong link between shame and addiction. Perhaps that's
because shame, like addiction, is at its core a rejection of our self.

To understand the corrosive effects of shame on our sense of
self, it's important to recognize the difference between shame and
guilt. The author John Bradshaw explained it this way: "Guilt says
I've done something wrong; shame says *there is something wrong
with me*. Guilt says I've made a mistake; shame says *I am a mistake.* Guilt says what I did was not good; shame says *I am no good.*"

Guilt, while an uncomfortable and often painful emotion, has
a healthy purpose in our life. It's a signal that we've crossed a social
or moral line by behaving in a hurtful, disrespectful, or dishonest
way. Guilt alerts us to our mistakes so we can learn, make amends,
and do better next time. Guilt does not diminish our worth as a
human being. Instead, it's a reflection of the fact that *we are human,* a re-affirmation of our capacity for growth and redemption.

Although guilt is usually attached to a particular action, shame
is all-encompassing, making us feel "less than" others and deny-

ing our fundamental worth as a human being. In our celebrity-obsessed culture, awash in images of physical perfection, shame can center on a perceived physical flaw, leading to self-critical thoughts such as "I'm too short" or "My thighs are too fat." Shame can also result from cultural prejudice about our race, religion, economic status, or sexual identity.

In its most toxic form, shame isn't limited to a particular aspect of our self. Instead, it's a more global feeling of self-loathing, the deep conviction that there's something irreparably wrong with us. Sometimes, this type of shame stems from harsh messages received in childhood. A friend of mine recalled, "I can still hear my grandmother's voice saying things like, 'Shame on you! You should be ashamed of yourself!' What a message to give a kid!" Shame can also result from childhood trauma such as parental neglect or abuse or chronic bullying. Since children usually blame themselves for painful events over which they have no control, they internalize the message that they are unworthy and unlovable.

Whatever its source, shame is so painful that it can lead to serious emotional problems including depression and anxiety—conditions that are associated with attempts to "self-medicate" through substance or behavioral addictions.

Furthermore, shame is often an underlying cause of anger. When we are constantly humiliated or belittled—when our basic human need for respect and acceptance is not met—it's natural to respond with anger. I know a woman who, after enduring years of psychological abuse from her husband, was told by her therapist, "Your anger is the healthy part of you."

It's true that anger can be an important signal that we need to make some changes in our life. It can motivate us to take necessary action. But when anger takes over and becomes our dominant emotion, the underlying unmet need for love and acceptance may go unrecognized. Instead, anger can divert attention away from the root problem and keep us stuck in an unhappy pattern of bitterness and resentment. It can even escalate into violence.

Psychiatrist James Gilligan has studied the link between shame and violence for more than thirty-five years. Working with inmates in prisons and prison mental hospitals, he concluded that most of the violent criminals he met had been abused or rejected by their parents, creating a pathological craving for acceptance and respect. Child abuse is "humiliating and shame-inducing," he wrote, because "it is the clearest possible way of communicating to the child that the parent does not love him [or her]." He continued:

> Just as pride means self-love (and its various synonyms, such as self-esteem, self-respect, or feelings of self-worth), shame means the lack or deficiency of self-love. There are only two possible sources of love for the self: from oneself and from others . . . And when the self is not loved, by itself or by another, it dies, just as surely as the body dies without oxygen.

As people in recovery, many of us have struggled to feel self-love. The shame of addiction, as well as the shame that may have preceded it, can make us believe that we don't deserve love, respect, acceptance, or happiness.

Such painful feelings of self-rejection come from the false assumption that our human imperfections make us unlovable. Our rational brain may recognize that this is not true. But releasing our shame emotionally usually takes a long time. That's because letting go of shame requires us to create a new narrative identity—one that is based on self-love rather than self-rejection. Redemption, not contamination.

"Shame is a soul-eating emotion," wrote Carl Jung. When we live our lives from a place of shame, it casts a shadow over everything we do. Because we believe we are unworthy, we get mired in self-defeating thoughts and behaviors that reinforce our negative self-image. In a sense, shame creates a false self—the object of our loathing—and prevents us from discovering the worthwhile being we really are.

Mindfulness shines the light of clarity through the darkness. We learn to pay attention to the stories we tell ourselves, challenging long-held beliefs with a simple question: "Is this true?" We begin to question preconceptions, to recognize that thoughts are only thoughts, and to practice skillful behaviors that support and nurture us. Most importantly, we remind ourselves again and again that we, no less than anyone, are deserving of love, acceptance, fulfillment, and happiness.

PRACTICE: **Relearning your loveliness.** "Everything flowers from within, of self-blessing; though sometimes it is necessary to reteach a thing its loveliness." This is the most-quoted line from the poem at the beginning of this chapter, and with good reason: self-blessing, or self-love, is the wellspring of all that is good within us. We can't give love and compassion to other living beings if we don't first give them to our self.

The Pali word *metta* means lovingkindness. Metta meditation is a focused practice that helps us develop love and compassion for our self and others. To begin, prepare as if for breathing meditation (as described in chapter 1's "Just Breathe" section) and get into a comfortable seated or reclining position. You may close your eyes or focus on a point in the distance.

When you are ready, quietly chant or think any or all of these metta phrases:

"May I be free from fear."
"May I be free from suffering."
"May I be happy."
"May I be filled with lovingkindness."

Select the phrase or phrases that mean the most to you. Repeat them over and over—perhaps for two or three minutes—even if you don't feel them. Even if you don't believe you are worthy. Plant the seeds of self-love within yourself, knowing that they will take root and blossom. *How can you carry self-blessing with you as you go about your day?*

The One We Feed

The Cherokee people tell the story of a young boy who was badly wronged by someone he considered a friend. The boy, hurt and furious, told his grandfather about the incident.

His grandfather nodded understandingly. "At times, I too have felt hatred for those who do great harm and seem to feel no sorrow about it. I have struggled with these feelings many times. It is as if two wolves live inside me. They live inside you, too.

"One wolf is good. He is peaceful, generous, compassionate, and wise. He lives in harmony with all those around him and does not easily take offense. He fights only when it is right to do so. But the other wolf lives in me as well—and in you. He is full of anger, envy, self-pity, and pain. The smallest obstacle infuriates him. He cannot think clearly because his anger is so great, yet that anger changes nothing. Sometimes it is hard to live with two wolves inside me, for both of them struggle to dominate my spirit."

The boy looked intently into his grandfather's eyes and asked, "Which wolf wins, grandfather?"

The grandfather smiled and said quietly, "The one I feed."

REFLECTION: "Do I contradict myself? Very well, then I Contradict myself, I am large, I contain multitudes," wrote the poet Walt Whitman. We all contain multitudes. *Among the multitude of contradictory thoughts and impulses inside you, which ones will you choose to feed?*

●

The Healing Light
of Compassion

Lord, make me an instrument of your peace:
Where there is hatred, let me sow love;
where there is injury, pardon;
where there is doubt, faith;
where there is despair, hope;
where there is darkness, light;
where there is sadness, joy.

O divine Master, grant that I may not so much seek
to be consoled as to console,
to be understood as to understand,
to be loved as to love.
For it is in giving that we receive,
it is in pardoning that we are pardoned,
and it is in dying that we are born to eternal life. Amen.

—Prayer of St. Francis

THERE'S A WELL-KNOWN STORY of a young mother whose only son fell ill and died when he was one year old. Distraught with grief, the woman carried her dead son to the Buddha and begged him to give her medicine to revive the child. The Buddha told the mother to go to every house in the village and gather a few mustard seeds from any family that had never known suffering. He promised to make the medicine from the seeds when she returned.

The desperate mother knocked on every door in the village in search of a family that had never known suffering, but she could not find one. In time, she discovered what the Buddha had wanted her to learn for herself—that suffering is part of life. It comes to everyone. With that new understanding, she was gradually able to accept and mourn her loss.

The woman learned an important lesson that we all learn sooner or later: life is a mixture of fortune and loss, of joy and sorrow. But beneath this basic truth lies a perplexing question: Why must we suffer?

It's a question as old as humanity itself.

Why Is There So Much Suffering?

We humans are unique in the animal kingdom (as far as we know) in that we have self-awareness. Look at a dog or a parrot or a squirrel, and you'll see a creature that doesn't give two hoots about its appearance or its accomplishments or the meaning of life. Most animals, if left to their own devices, are blessed with the ability to simply *be.* Like Adam and Eve before the fall, they have a childlike innocence of sin or pretense or loss or death.

Our more complicated brain gives us a higher level of consciousness, which allows us to conceptualize not only our own existence but also the past, the future, and the boundless universe. We are, in a very real sense, privileged witnesses to the vast cosmic mystery.

In another sense, though, we humans carry a unique burden. Alone among the animals (again, as far as we know), we are aware that we and everyone we love will die. In almost every culture throughout history, that knowledge has inspired spiritual beliefs, practices, and rituals designed to ease the pain of our own mortality.

But death, while perhaps our primal sorrow, is far from being our only sorrow. Heartache and tragedy are woven into the human saga, and most of the world's major belief systems have developed complex ideologies in response. Christianity and Buddhism, for example, devote considerable attention to the cause and purpose of human suffering. As might be expected, each offers a somewhat different perspective.

Suffering is a central theme of Christianity, as punishment for sin but also as a path to salvation. According to the Bible, Adam and Eve brought sin and suffering to the world when they disobeyed God's command. For their transgression, God punished them and their descendants, saying, "I will greatly multiply thy sorrow . . . in sorrow shalt thou eat of [the ground] all the days of thy life; thorns also and thistles shall it bring forth to thee."

However, Christian doctrine does not teach that suffering is purely punitive. God uses suffering to test, teach, and guide humans to a higher level of perfection. This is illustrated in the story of Job, a sinless man who retains his faith in God despite suffering a succession of calamities. "Though he slay me, yet I will trust in him," says Job.

Although we may not know the reason for our suffering, Christianity teaches, we must endure with patience and trust in God's wisdom. As a reward, we will be reunited with God in the afterlife and all suffering will end.

In Buddhism, suffering is linked not to a deity but to human nature—specifically to our attachment to impermanent things (and everything is impermanent). In tough times, we forget that our troubles are temporary. We increase our suffering because we fixate on our pain, overlooking the fact that more agreeable experiences are sure to come. Similarly, when we cling to external rewards that we think will make us happy—money, success, fame, or romance—we can never be satisfied. We live in fear of losing what we have, or we long to acquire more and more, always seeking that magic something to fulfill our bottomless desire.

Buddhism teaches that pleasure and pain come and go like the changing seasons. Being attached to one or the other creates needless suffering, and the only way to avoid it is to accept life as it is. As Lao-Tzu put it:

> Be content with what you have;
> Rejoice in the way things are.
> When you realize there is nothing lacking,
> The whole world belongs to you.

Although Christianity and Buddhism view suffering from different perspectives—one counsels trust in the wisdom of God; the other advocates letting go of human desire—both advise acceptance in the face of pain as well as a willingness to learn from suffering.

> **REFLECTION:** "All the suffering, stress, and addiction comes from not realizing you already are what you are looking for," wrote Jon Kabat-Zinn. *If you can be content with things as they are just for today, will you suffer less?*

Finding Meaning in Pain

The year I turned forty, my husband of twenty-two years left me for an eighteen-year-old girl. She was a high school classmate of my two older children, and he was her teacher. I was beyond devastated. I didn't think I'd survive. For months I felt as if I couldn't breathe. I wept on the way to and from work and again at night when the kids were asleep. I felt lost and disoriented, like I'd stumbled into a terrifying, hostile country. I simply didn't know how to live without him. There was no "me," there had only been "us," and now that was gone.

Today, more than twenty years later, thinking about that chapter of my life can still make me sad. Sometimes I even cry a little. But mostly, I think about how that experience set me on a long and difficult path to recovering *me,* the self I had lost almost without noticing. Like many people, I gradually saw that intense suffering can sometimes light the way toward personal growth.

Suffering is something we instinctively wish to avoid. When difficult emotions bubble up or when we experience physical pain, we automatically look for something to distract or soothe us. Freud called this response the "pleasure principle," theorizing that we all seek to attain pleasure and avoid pain.

Yet most of us have willingly suffered at one point or another in pursuit of an important goal. Athletes put themselves through grueling workouts to improve their performance. Women endure the pain of childbirth to bring new life into the world. And anyone who has gone through withdrawal knows that prolonged suffering is sometimes a necessary step toward a better life.

When we suffer for a purpose, we find meaning in our pain, making it easier to bear. But what about suffering we don't choose? What about losing a loved one or being diagnosed with a serious illness or living each day with soul-numbing depression? How do we find meaning in those crushing experiences?

Philosophers and spiritual leaders have had much to say on the topic. Most have concurred with Aristotle's assertion that "learning is not child's play; we cannot learn without pain." In the Bible's book of Romans, we read, "[W]e also glory in our sufferings because we know that suffering produces perseverance; perseverance, character; and character, hope." The Dalai Lama wrote, "It is under the greatest adversity that there exists the greatest potential for doing good, both for oneself and others."

And the eighth-century Buddhist monk Shantideva taught that suffering can lead to wisdom in three important ways: First, suffering can chase out arrogance and replace it with humility, which opens our mind to life's deeper lessons. Second, it can expand our compassion for others who suffer, deepening our understanding of the human condition. And third, it can inspire us to lead a virtuous life. After all, when we obey laws, live with integrity, and treat others with respect, we reduce the suffering caused by our own unskillful behaviors.

The underlying message is not that we should try to suffer more so we can become better people. The message is that we can learn important lessons from suffering—when we are ready and if we are willing to listen.

✳

Many years ago, I became friendly with a woman who was suffering from major depression. Getting through each day was an ordeal, and life seemed utterly meaningless to her. I discovered that she had lost her nursing license a few years earlier because of drug use. There were steps she could take to get it back, but they involved two or three years of drug testing, which meant she'd have to stop smoking marijuana.

"Pot's the only thing that helps me through the day," she moaned. "It's the one pleasure I have left." On the other hand, she knew in her heart that she was born to be a nurse. That was her true calling. She wrestled with the problem for a long time, trying to figure out which was worse—the deprivation of giving up pot, or the sadness of missing her calling. Finally, she realized that her depression was telling her to get her nursing license back. Today, she's a practicing nurse, and while she still has bouts of depression, she's generally content with her life because it once again has purpose and meaning.

Her story is not unusual. Many of us stay in unhappy situations because we're afraid of what we'll suffer if we try to change. But fear of suffering can in itself become a source of pain, depriving us of the ability to live fully. As the Trappist monk Thomas Merton wrote, "Indeed, the truth that many people never understand, until it is too late, is that the more you try to avoid suffering, the more you suffer."

It may seem paradoxical, but accepting pain as an inevitable part of life is perhaps the best way to *reduce* our suffering. With acceptance, we begin to open our heart to lessons we have yet to learn.

> **REFLECTION:** "Grief can be the garden of compassion. If you keep your heart open through everything, your pain can become your greatest ally in your life's search for love and wisdom." These words from the thirteenth-century Persian poet Rumi remind us that there are lessons to be learned from suffering. *What can your suffering teach you?*

What's Compassion Got to Do with It?

It's hard to argue with the notion that suffering can be a gateway to wisdom. The idea is so entrenched in our consciousness that we readily accept clichés like "sadder but wiser" and "no pain, no gain." But suffering in itself is of no benefit until we are ready to learn from it—a process that can take a very long time. What's more, we can't make the leap from suffering to wisdom without first spending some time in the "garden of compassion," in Rumi's words.

Compassion is the quality that allows us to see things from another's perspective. Rooted in the experience of our own pain, compassion opens our eyes to the reality that everyone is subject to adversity and loss. It helps us move past the judgmentalism and narrow-mindedness that distort our worldview and it fosters a higher understanding of the interconnected nature of existence.

Ultimately, compassion is the deepest expression of our

shared humanity, combining sympathy—"I'm sorry for your suffering"—and empathy—"I feel your pain"—with a genuine desire to ease suffering whenever we encounter it—"Let me do my best to help." It's the motivation behind the comforting word to someone who's hurting, the helping hand for someone in need.

For those of us in recovery, compassion is of particular importance in our journey toward self-knowledge. Addiction is an intensely isolating disease, focusing our attention almost exclusively on our inner sensations of pleasure or pain. When we're addicted, we have little regard for the feelings of others. We justify our actions based on how we feel at any given moment, and we prioritize our relationships based on what others can do for us—on whether they'll help or impede the gratification of our needs.

Adding further to our isolation is the shame that inevitably accompanies addiction. We feel separate from "normal" people, cut off from the mainstream of society and cast into the role of "misfit" or "loser." Feeling both isolated and ashamed, we fail to truly connect with others in any meaningful way. Even in recovery we often feel lonely, rejected, and misunderstood.

Compassion can help us cope with these painful emotions and bridge the gulf between our self and others. When we practice compassion, we discover that we are not alone in our suffering, that through our suffering we are linked with the rest of humanity, and that, in the words of Mother Teresa, "If we have no peace, it is because we have forgotten that we belong to each other."

Compassion allows us to see the world in a kinder, gentler light. We don't blind ourselves to human flaws and absurdities. We don't pretend that ignorance and cruelty don't exist. Instead, we try to look past human error to see the suffering person inside —the one who, like everyone on earth, must cope with worry, regret, loneliness, and loss.

> **PRACTICE: Lovingkindness.** "Be kind, for everyone you meet is fighting a harder battle," wrote Plato more than twenty-three hundred years ago. In this version of metta (lovingkindness) meditation, we'll build our capacity for compassion by directing thoughts of love and compassion toward others.
>
> To begin, sit as for breathing meditation or lie down comfortably on your back. Your eyes may be open or closed. Breathe normally. When you are ready, direct thoughts of lovingkindness toward yourself by quietly, slowly saying any or all of these metta phrases and bringing your full attention to the meaning of each word:
>
> > **"May I be free from fear."**
> > **"May I be free from suffering."**
> > **"May I be happy."**
> > **"May I be filled with lovingkindness."**
>
> Now, think of someone you know who is having a difficult time. Picture the person's face. Say his or her name. Direct thoughts of lovingkindness toward that person by softly saying the metta phrases you choose:
>
> > **"May you be free from fear."**
> > **"May you be free from suffering."**
> > **"May you be happy."**
> > **"May you be filled with lovingkindness."**
>
> Continue to focus on the meaning of the words until you are ready to end your meditation. *How can you carry those feelings of lovingkindness with you today?*

Difficult Relationships

We humans are social creatures. Our species would not have survived without the cooperative interdependence of our earliest ancestors. We thrived and multiplied because—despite the spectacular destructiveness of wars and other acts of violence—we shared our ideas, knowledge, and resources. Today, even if we imagine ourselves to be totally independent, we're sustained by a complex social and economic network of production, services, and technology.

Simply put, we need each other. But our need goes much deeper than mere survival. We depend on others for spiritual and emotional sustenance. Our need for connection is so great that babies can die from lack of affection. Parental coldness can lead to learning and behavioral problems in children. Social isolation—the lack of meaningful social support (a condition that affects about 25 percent of Americans)—has been linked to physical and mental illnesses including major depression and addiction.

But even though relationships are vital to our well-being, they can also be a source of conflict and pain. When demanding bosses, grumpy coworkers, annoying neighbors, and difficult relatives make us feel miserable, how does compassion come into the picture?

Quite simply, difficult relationships, like suffering itself, expand our opportunities to practice compassion. Compassion has nothing to do with whether we like or approve of someone. When people treat us badly or behave in cruel or unethical ways, it's perfectly legitimate to recognize their dangers and protect ourselves from the harm they might cause. At the same time, we can offer compassion, knowing that they, too, have experienced suffering. As the Dalai Lama explained:

> Sometimes we think that to develop an open heart, to be truly loving and compassionate, means that we need to be passive, to allow others to abuse us, to smile and let anyone do what they want with us. Yet this is not what is meant by compassion. Quite the contrary. Compassion is not at all weak. It is the strength that arises out of seeing the true nature of suffering in the world. Compassion allows us to bear witness to that suffering, whether it is in ourselves or others, without fear; it allows us to name injustice without hesitation, and to act strongly, with all the skill at our disposal.

When we deal with people who are chronically harsh, angry, judgmental, or demanding, we're at risk of absorbing some of their misery. Our challenge is to act honorably and keep our equilibrium while recognizing the inner turmoil behind their behavior. We can sincerely wish them to be free of pain and at the same time do what we must to defend ourselves from the havoc they create. This can mean limiting our contact with them, practicing mini-meditations to offset their negativity, or calmly asserting our right to not be abused.

Whatever strategies we adopt, they're likely to work better when they're grounded in compassion. When we offer compassion without first deciding who is and who isn't worthy of our generous spirit, we begin to think less in terms of "us" and "them" and more in terms of our shared humanity.

This kind of awareness can enhance all our relationships, including those with difficult people we happen to love. It can also help us build compassionate awareness of difficult qualities within our self.

"Everything that irritates us about others can lead us to an understanding of ourselves," observed Carl Jung. That truth came home to me a few years ago when I worked in a corporate setting for a woman I disliked intensely. My boss was demanding and aloof and exuded an aura of supreme self-assurance. A lot of people in the company found her hard to deal with, but my feelings went further than that. An encounter with her could completely ruin my day. I began to dread going to work.

I couldn't understand why my reactions to her were so much stronger than my coworkers', so I talked the situation over with a counselor. She helped me see that my boss displayed qualities I'd learned to suppress in myself—assertiveness, confidence, and a sense of self-worth. The solution to my workplace dilemma was not to try to change my boss's style but to work on qualities I wanted to develop in myself and learn to express them in my own way.

When we take the time to analyze what it is about someone that triggers a strong negative response, we sometimes discover uncomfortable but important truths about our self. The father who is disturbed by his son's lack of athleticism may be projecting his own sense of vulnerability. The mother who is upset by her daughter's eating habits could herself be struggling with body image. The sister who labels her successful brother a "snob" may be trying to hide her own feelings of inferiority.

In some ways, our relationships are a mirror of our sense

of self. The more fraught they are, the more they reflect back to us our own inner struggles. Although it can be hard to face our less-than-admirable traits, we can't begin to address them until we do. Denial has never solved anything. By seeing and accepting our own difficult qualities, we can stop pretending they don't exist. Instead, we can offer compassion to our self, just as we offer it to others, knowing that compassionate self-awareness is key to personal growth.

> **REFLECTION:** "When you struggle with your partner, you are struggling with yourself," wrote Deepak Chopra. "Every fault you see in them touches a denied weakness in yourself." *What can you learn about yourself from the difficult people in your life?*

Choosing Forgiveness

Nelson Mandela was once asked what he felt toward his jailers when he was freed after twenty-seven years of unjust imprisonment. "I was angry. And I was a little afraid," he responded. "After all, I'd not been free in so long." He reflected for a moment and added, "But when I felt that anger welling up inside me, I realized that if I continue to hate them after I got outside that gate, then they would still have me. I wanted to be free, so I let it go."

I wanted to be free. Mandela's words reflect an important truth: that resentment and anger make us prisoners of the past. To be truly free of the harm that others have done to us—and that we have done to others—we must learn to forgive. But what exactly does forgiveness mean, and how do we get there? One way to start is with intention.

Forgiveness is a choice. It's an intentional decision to change our emotional response to a hurt we have suffered. Although some of the work of forgiveness may happen subconsciously—that is, the cumulative effects of time and experience may soften the pain of the injury—resentment and anger are likely to linger unless we consciously choose to forgive.

Making that choice does not come quickly or easily for most of us. Instead, it's usually a complex process of sorting through difficult feelings of denial, hurt, anger, and sorrow before eventually reaching a place of acceptance and release. When we choose to forgive, it doesn't mean that we excuse, condone, forget, or deny the injury we have suffered. We don't try to pretend that a wrong wasn't done. It simply means that we learn to let go of anger and resentment so we can heal from the past and be at peace in the present.

I once met an elderly woman who seemed to epitomize this truth. She told me that her daughter had been murdered at the age of thirteen many years earlier. Yet she had gradually found a way to forgive the murderer. She did it, she said, because she wanted her memories of her daughter to be filled with love and joy, not with rage and grief. "The angrier I was, the farther away from me she was," the woman explained. "I was so full of darkness there was no room for her inside me. I had to let go of my anger to make room for her. Now, I carry her here in my heart."

In her wisdom, she understood that forgiveness is less about the person who committed the wrong and more about our self. When we forgive an injury, the past hurt loses its power over us. We accept that something wrong—sometimes something *terrible*—has happened, and it's never going to change. But we choose not to carry it with us anymore. We decide to let anger go so we can find peace in our heart.

✳

While forgiveness is basically about accepting what happened and letting go of anger, compassion can play an important role in moving the process forward.

Many spiritual traditions, including Christianity, point to compassion as a basis for forgiveness. "And forgive us our trespasses, as we forgive those who trespass against us," states the Lord's Prayer. And as he was dying in agony on the cross, Jesus cried out, "Father forgive them, for they know not what they do."

These sentiments spring from the recognition that both the offender and the victim are imperfect beings, subject to the fears, ignorance, confusion, and weaknesses of the human condition. They underscore the reality that all humans experience suffering in one way or another, an understanding that can light the path to forgiveness. This is something a friend experienced firsthand. He said that for years he'd harbored resentment against his mother for staying with his abusive father. He kept telling himself that she should have just left him.

"But after I did a lot of work on myself, I started seeing things differently," he told me. "Here was a woman with a fifth-grade education, chronic heart problems, no job skills, no money, no confidence, and nowhere to turn for support. I realized that she'd done the best she could. She probably suffered a lot in silence."

He paused before adding, "Once I started putting myself in her shoes, I felt a lot of compassion for her. It's allowed me to become closer to her."

Many of us who have struggled with addiction have been deeply wounded, sometimes by the people we trusted most. Abuse, neglect, betrayal, and injustice are common threads in our personal histories. In meetings, we share stories of chaotic childhoods, parental conflict, ruined holidays, and broken promises. "My house was like the Wild West," one man recalled.

As adults, we may come to believe that continued anger is our only way to protest the wrongs that we suffered. We fear that by letting go of our anger, the injury will be forgotten. Yet anger does nothing to remedy the past. It only prolongs our suffering. And to forgive does not mean to forget, as the author Barbara Kingsolver noted: "Listen. Slide the weight from your shoulders and move forward. You are afraid you might forget, but you never will. You will forgive and remember."

Because forgiveness requires us to deal with deep and upsetting emotions, it can be helpful to think of it as a process rather than as a fixed state of mind. We move forward at our own pace and in our own way, knowing that as we "slide the weight from our shoulders," we free ourselves to create a fuller, more contented life.

PRACTICE: **Walking awareness.** Being present in our body is a useful way to break a chain of painful thoughts. In walking meditation, we focus on lifting first one foot and then the other. Outdoors is best, or you can use a large indoor space with room for about twenty paces before you need to turn around.

Start by aligning your body in good standing posture. You should be comfortable, not rigid, with your spine straight and feet about shoulder-width apart. As you begin to walk, do so at a normal pace. Notice the feelings in your feet, legs, pelvis, torso, arms, neck, and head as you move. Notice how perfectly the parts of your body work together. If you have discomfort or distracting thoughts, simply note them without judgment. Then bring your attention back to your body.

Continue in this manner for as long as you like—perhaps starting with five minutes the first time and working your way up to ten or twenty. *How does being present in your body free you from thoughts about the past?*

Why Self-Compassion Matters

"Finish each day and be done with it. You have done what you could. Some blunders and absurdities no doubt crept in; forget them as soon as you can. Tomorrow is a new day; begin it well and serenely and with too high a spirit to be encumbered with your old nonsense."

More than a hundred years ago, Ralph Waldo Emerson wrote those words to one of his daughters who was troubled by a mistake she had made at school. Today, his fatherly advice is in keeping with a growing body of research into the impact of self-compassion on our well-being. Psychologists and social scientists increasingly agree that being kind to our self plays a crucial role in helping us achieve our goals and live a happier, healthier life.

To understand why self-compassion is so important, it's useful to consider two well-known factors in our sense of self: self-criticism and self-esteem.

Most of us are well acquainted with self-criticism. It's the nasty little voice inside our head that says we're stupid. We're ugly. Nobody likes us. We're not good enough.

It's our automatic response to an awkward moment ("I'm such a klutz!") or an honest mistake ("I'm such a loser!") or a glimpse of ourselves in a storefront window ("I'm so fat!"). Self-criticism can run so deep that it becomes the soundtrack of our life, sort of like bad background music in a department store—always there but scarcely noticed. Yet it has an enormously negative impact on our mental and physical health.

In one social psychology research review, the authors concluded that habitual self-critics have a hard time achieving goals because they are likely to obsess about "real or perceived failure," to be hypersensitive to perceived criticism, and to focus more on "avoiding failure and preventing potential loss of self-esteem than on effective goal pursuit." What's more, they said, habitual self-criticism is consistently linked with "impaired functioning, lower satisfaction and well-being, and various forms of pathological functioning, such as depression, anxiety, and obsessive-compulsive syndromes."

But the harmful effects of self-criticism go even deeper. When we attack our self with negative messages, our body activates the stress hormones that are part of its natural response to danger. Elevated levels of these hormones have been linked to heart disease, high blood pressure, digestive disorders, immune system problems, diabetes—even cancer.

Nevertheless, many of us continuously beat ourselves up because that's what feels "normal." We may have internalized harsh messages we received from others. Or we may believe—as lots of people do—that if we don't feel attractive, successful, rich, or happy enough, the solution is to be harder on our self. In the words of Dr. Kristin Neff, an expert on the subject, "The reason people aren't more self-compassionate is that they are afraid they'll become self-indulgent. They believe self-criticism is what keeps them in line. Most people have gotten it wrong because our culture says being hard on yourself is the way to be."

Yet self-critical thoughts do nothing to help us solve problems or achieve the changes we wish to make. Instead, self-criticism keeps us stuck in an endless loop of negative messages and self-defeating behaviors.

If self-criticism is so bad for us, then self-esteem must be terrific, right? Well, yes and no. Self-esteem is related to our overall sense of self. Healthy self-esteem means that we believe in our own worth and in our ability to function competently in the world. Low self-esteem means that we devalue our self and doubt our ideas and abilities. Excessive—and therefore unhealthy—self-esteem means that we feel superior to others.

Clearly, healthy self-esteem is an asset that can improve our quality of life. But it can be easily shattered. A job loss, relationship break-up, serious illness, or financial disaster can turn our confidence on its head. Furthermore, our self-esteem often suffers when we compare ourselves to people who seem to be doing better than we are. For example, studies have shown that looking at pictures of happy families on social media can make us feel worse about our own situation in life.

On the other hand, while low self-esteem is characteristic of people who experience addiction, traditional methods of psychotherapy have had limited success in helping clients make the leap from low to healthy self-esteem. That's because changing our self-image is usually a long and complicated process.

More recently, research has shown that learning to treat our self with compassion can be more beneficial than trying to *earn* ourselves more self-esteem.

Self-compassion combines three important skills: paying attention to our painful thoughts and emotions (mindfulness), recognizing that all people struggle (connection), and treating our self with kindness (compassion).

In practice, self-compassion means that when we have a self-critical thought—"Of course I didn't get the job! I'm a loser!" —we bring the thought out of our subconscious and notice it without judgment. We remember that a thought is just a thought. Then we mentally connect with others, reminding our self that everyone struggles with failure and feelings of inadequacy. That's part of being human. Finally, we offer our self the same loving-kindness we would offer a cherished friend or relative who is suffering.

To test the effectiveness of this approach, self-compassion skills were taught to ninth graders in a large study published in 2014. It found that "self-compassion protects against the negative effects of low self-esteem." Even if students who received self-compassion training continued to have self-critical thoughts, those thoughts had little effect on their sense of well-being compared to students who had not learned self-compassion skills. Self-compassion, it seems, offsets the blows to self-image that come with disappointment and failure.

A friend of mine has seen the value of self-compassion in her struggle to control her weight. "It was a vicious cycle," she said. "I'd binge, beat myself up about it, and then eat even more as a kind of self-punishment. Now when I slip up, I remind myself that I'm still a worthwhile person. I try to let go of those hateful thoughts and give myself kindness, instead. It helps."

And that's self-compassion in a nutshell: We accept that we're flawed. We admit that we're disappointed in ourselves. And we try to do better. But we do so within a context of understanding and kindness toward our self. As psychologist Steven C. Hayes noted:

> It's time for us to put down the idea that we have to think well of ourselves at all times to be mature, successful, functional, mentally healthy individuals. Indeed, this toxic idea can foster a kind of narcissistic, ego-based self-story that is bound to blow up on us. Instead of increasing self-esteem *content* what we need to do is increase self-compassion as the *context* of all we do . . . we all have self-doubt, we all suffer, we all fail from time to time, but none of that means we can't live a life of meaning, purpose, and compassion for ourselves and others.

Self-compassion requires us to develop a new relationship with our self—to become, in effect, our own best friend. By accepting our imperfections, acknowledging our suffering, and understanding that we share these traits with all of humanity, we can begin to give our self what we have always longed for: acceptance, kindness, and unconditional love.

In the words of the Dalai Lama, "If you want others to be happy, practice compassion. If you want to be happy, practice compassion."

PRACTICE: Change your life. "A moment of self-compassion can change your entire day. A string of such moments can change the course of your life," wrote psychologist Christopher K. Germer. Try journaling as a form of meditation to explore the concept of self-compassion. To begin, find a quiet place where you'll be undisturbed for ten or fifteen minutes. Using pen and paper or a keyboard—whatever you prefer—fill an entire page with your thoughts on self-compassion. Here are some ideas to consider: *What does self-compassion mean to you? What negative self-talk would you have to give up to be more self-compassionate? How can you practice self-compassion today? How can moments of self-compassion improve your life?*

5

The Beacon of Virtue

Abandon wrongdoing.

It can be done.

If there were no likelihood, I would not ask you to do it.

But since it is possible

and since it brings blessing and happiness,

I do ask of you:

abandon wrongdoing.

Cultivate doing good.

It can be done.

If it brought deprivation and sorrow, I would not ask
you to do it.

But since it brings blessing and happiness,

I do ask of you:

cultivate doing good.

—The Buddha

IN DECEMBER 1915—more than a year after the start of World War I and nearly three years before the end of that bloody conflagration—British and German soldiers called a Christmas Day truce. It followed a similar truce that had taken place the year before, when opposing troops on the Western Front had spontaneously sung carols together, exchanged gifts, and allowed each other time to recover and bury their dead friends. But this year, orders prohibiting such conduct had come down from top brass on both sides of the conflict. Fraternizing with the enemy for any reason—including the observance of Christmas—was treasonous.

As Christmas approached that winter, commanding officers tried to enforce the directive. But soldiers defied their superiors and ignored the order. Author Llewelyn Wyn Griffith wrote that men called out to each other across the trenches, "Merry Christmas, Tommy!" and "Merry Christmas, Fritz!" He described the scene that unfolded:

> As soon as it became light, we saw hands and bottles being waved at us, with encouraging shouts that we could neither understand nor misunderstand. A drunken German stumbled over his parapet and advanced through the barbed wire, followed by several others, and in a few moments there was a rush of men from both sides, carrying tins of meat, biscuits, and other odd commodities for barter.

This second truce—an outpouring of human generosity amid the senseless barbarity of war—is particularly noteworthy because ordinary soldiers risked severe punishment to do what they thought was right. By offering fellowship and goodwill to men who were supposed to be their enemies, they followed a higher moral principle centered on kindness and generosity—the very essence of the Christmas spirit. They also exemplified the courage it can sometimes take to live in harmony with our deepest values.

Since values form an important part of our personal identity, it's worth thinking about what they are and how they affect our quality of life.

The Values-Happiness Connection

When I was young and inexperienced and more than a little rebellious, I never gave much thought to what makes a satisfying life. I lived each day as it came, and if the day included a few drinks and some laughs, so much the better. I certainly didn't think about values. But if I'd been asked to name some principles that were important to me, I probably would have said something about freedom, individuality, and being able to do what I wanted.

For me, being an adult was all about asserting my right to be myself—which might have been okay if I hadn't been so unaware of who I really was. It took a lot of years and a lot of floundering for me to figure out what truly mattered to me. As with many people, it came down to family and friends, satisfying work, and finding a sense of purpose.

Indeed, study after study has shown that these are the building blocks of lasting happiness. But what's often left unsaid is the fact that our success in these areas depends to a great extent on our personal values. After all, our values—that is, our beliefs about what is right or wrong, acceptable or unacceptable, and important or unimportant—drive the choices we make in just about every area of our life. In a sense, our values are the invisible hand that shapes the life we create for our self. As Mahatma Gandhi put it:

> Your beliefs become your thoughts,
> Your thoughts become your words,
> Your words become your actions,
> Your actions become your habits,
> Your habits become your values,
> Your values become your destiny.

How do values become destiny? Quite simply, the value we attach to things like family, friendships, education, health, or material success determines the amount of time and attention we're willing to spend on them. If we place a high value on family and friendships, for example, we may try to do our best to nurture them. Similarly, if we believe that material success is important, we may be motivated to work hard to achieve it.

Intangibles such as status, security, spirituality, or independence also have value and affect the choices we make. For example, people who strongly value security may be reluctant to take risks, while those who place a higher value on independence might walk away from a safe situation that's become too restrictive. And those who value spirituality above status may choose a contemplative life and forgo opportunities for advancement in the workplace.

The point is that whether we're aware of them or not, our values guide us toward certain paths and away from others. When we pay attention to what actually matters to us—as opposed to what society says *should* matter to us—we're better able to make life choices that are in keeping with who we truly are.

Henry David Thoreau, perhaps more than any other writer, exemplified what it is to live in harmony with our deepest values. He perplexed many of his contemporaries when he rejected the pursuit of material wealth and chose, instead, to live as simply and purposefully as possible. He was guided by two core values: to be fully awake to every moment of his life and to be true to himself. He explained his unconventional lifestyle this way: "If a man does not keep pace with his companions, perhaps it is because he hears a different drummer. Let him step to the music he hears, however measured or far away."

The "drummer" for each of us is our personal values. When we act in step with what's important to us, we conduct ourselves in ways that bring greater satisfaction, meaning, and happiness to our life.

> **REFLECTION:** "Happiness is when what you think, what you say, and what you do are in harmony," wrote Mahatma Gandhi. *To what extent is what you think, believe, and value in harmony with what you do?*

Lighting a Moral Path

Values apply to just about every aspect of our life: How important do I think it is to take care of my health? To keep a clean house? To hone my job skills? To be a conscientious employee? To be of service to my community?

But *moral* values relate specifically to our ideas about right and wrong.

Philosophers as far back as Plato have argued that to be truly happy, we must be moral. That's because having a good moral character lays the foundation for a satisfying life. Qualities such as integrity, courage, self-discipline, and generosity allow us to build stable relationships, foster self-worth, and find meaning and purpose.

What's more, moral values can serve as a guiding light through life's inevitable storms. When we know what we stand for, our choices become clearer. But what exactly are "good" moral values, and how do we acquire them? Modern research offers some intriguing answers to these age-old questions.

Primatologist Frans de Waal has devoted decades to the study of primate social behavior. Early in his career, when he focused on competition and aggression, he was surprised to learn that chimpanzees intentionally reconcile after a fight. That discovery sparked an interest in moral behavior in animals, including humans.

What he and other researchers have consistently found is that certain traits associated with morality—cooperation, fairness, and caring about the well-being of others—seem to be innate in most mammals, including primates, elephants, and canines. Apes and monkeys, for example, hug and comfort peers who are upset, help each other complete tasks, and return favors for help they've received. They also have a strong sense of justice, as demonstrated in a well-known experiment showing that monkeys get upset if they're rewarded with cucumbers when their companions get grapes (a more desirable reward) for completing the same task. *What's good for one should be good for all,* they seem to be saying.

Although human moral behavior is more multilayered than that exhibited by other members of the animal kingdom, the significant point is that a bias toward morality seems to be written into our DNA. Many of the religious teachings, laws, and social norms that regulate societies around the globe are an expression of our natural moral instincts.

Furthermore, most of our ideas about morality are based on a few key concepts—what de Waal calls the "pillars of morality": "One is reciprocity, and associated with it is a sense of justice and a sense of fairness. And the other one is empathy and compassion."

Still, despite the fact that we seem to be born with moral tendencies—that is, we instinctively favor justice and compassion —moral growth is neither inevitable nor easy. We grow morally only through a combination of awareness, intention, effort, and practice.

Psychologists have observed that moral development usually progresses through several predictable stages. In early childhood, it's all about obedience and punishment. When we follow the rules, we're "good." When we don't, we're "bad." As our world expands, we're increasingly influenced by social norms and expectations. We learn to be "nice," to do our duty, and to respect authority. With growing maturity, we grapple with concepts of social responsibility and individual rights. We recognize the importance of law and order while also developing our own personal moral code—principles we value even if they conflict with society's rules.

Of course, few of us follow this pattern exactly, and the moral values we hold as adults can change with time and experience, says psychologist Richard Weissbourd:

Many adults, to be sure, change very little in the course of adulthood. There are narcissistic adults who never develop any real capacity to understand others, and there are adults whose compassion and integrity remain steady and deep throughout life. But to imagine moral character as unchanging is to grossly misunderstand the nature of most adults' lives ...

While many of us lose our ideals over time, others of us do not develop serious ideals until well into midlife. Some adults become wiser, more able to discern important moral truths; others' notions of fairness become more formulaic and coarse. Some adults become more selfish while others become more altruistic ...

[I]t is often not until well into adulthood that we tend to develop our most important qualities, including empathy for many kinds of people leading many kinds of lives, the capacity to love others despite their flaws, the ability to shield others from our destructive qualities, the ability to appreciate our ancestors and to plan for our descendants.

In other words, our moral values are not fixed. As adults, we have the power to determine our own moral path, which can be one of regression, stagnation, or growth. It's up to us.

As people in recovery, many of us can look back on regrettable choices we made during the course of our addictions and compulsions—choices that violated personal and social standards of right and wrong. After all, dishonesty in all its forms is a hallmark of addiction. But as Weissbourd makes clear, we retain the potential for moral growth throughout our lifetime. It is never too late to become a better person.

Mindfulness is a useful and practical tool for raising awareness of our self as a moral being. Regardless of our past, when we nurture the natural goodness within us, we lay the foundation for a future defined by integrity, generosity, and resilience. As the civil rights leader Whitney Young said: "There is nothing noble in being superior to someone else. The only real nobility is in being superior to your former self."

> **REFLECTION:** "Principles are to people what roots are to trees," wrote the nineteenth-century Spanish author Carlos Reyles. "Without roots, trees fall when they are thrashed with the winds of the pampas. Without principles, people fall when they are shaken by the gales of existence." *What are the "roots" or moral principles you wish to develop in yourself?*

The Eightfold Path

I once had the privilege of observing the creation of a sand mandala by a team of Tibetan Buddhist monks. They were visiting a college where I was teaching and had been allotted a bright, multi-windowed conference room for their work. For about two weeks, the monks in their flowing maroon robes labored silently over the large table, using tiny tools to place grains of colored sand in a geometric pattern, expanding from the center outward. I, along with many students and colleagues, stopped by frequently to watch the progress.

What slowly emerged was an intricate five-foot-square design featuring symbols and representations of deities unfamiliar to me. I marveled at the skill and precision required to compose such a beautiful work of art. When the mandala was complete, I marveled even more as the monks swept it into a container, the image destroyed and the mingled grains of sand destined for dispersal in flowing water at some later date. The entire process, I learned, had deep spiritual meaning for the monks, related to enlightenment, healing energies, and the impermanence of existence.

This experience was my first glimpse into Buddhism, which seemed rather mysterious and otherworldly to me. It would take me many years to discover that, far from being impractical, passive, or disconnected (misperceptions I held for a long time), Buddhism offers useful tools for leading a richer, more satisfying life.

Chief among them is the Eightfold Path, a practical framework for moral behavior. As its name implies, the Eightfold Path —or simply "the path"—focuses on eight aspects of moral conduct: Right View, Right Intention, Right Speech, Right Action, Right Livelihood, Right Effort, Right Mindfulness, and Right Concentration. (The term *right* means skillful or wholesome as well as nonharmful.) All are grouped into three broad categories: wisdom, ethical conduct, and mental discipline.

Like the Twelve Steps, the Eightfold Path is a guide to moral growth and a happier way of life. But there are important distinctions between the two approaches.

For one thing, the Steps are meant to be taken in order (although we return to earlier Steps again and again), but the Eightfold Path is more like a circle or a web. It's common in Twelve

The Eightfold Path
and its three parts

Wisdom Path	**Right View** Letting go of our delusions and misperceptions so we can see the world as it really is and better understand the true nature of reality.
	Right Intention Aligning our thoughts and purpose with moral principles before we speak or act.
Ethical Conduct Path	**Right Speech** Communicating in a thoughtful, honest, compassionate way.
	Right Action Conducting ourselves in ways that manifest truthfulness, responsibility, integrity, and compassion.
	Right Livelihood Making a living in ethical ways that cause no harm to our self or other living beings.
Mental Discipline Path	**Right Effort** Letting go of unskillful qualities such as greed, anger, and ignorance and cultivating skillful qualities such as generosity, lovingkindness, and wisdom.
	Right Mindfulness Being present in the moment and letting go of worries, daydreams, and distractions that prevent us from being fully awake.
	Right Concentration Learning to focus our mind through meditation or other dedicated practices.

Step recovery to focus solely on the first three Steps until we feel ready to move on, but we can enter the Eightfold Path at any point. Each interconnected part has its own focus but also supports the other parts.

Another difference is that the Steps advise us to seek guidance from a higher power while the path encourages us to search for wisdom within our self. "When making moral choices, individuals are advised to examine their motivation . . . and to weigh the consequences of their actions in light of the Buddha's teachings," explains the Tibetan Buddhist nun and theologian Karma Lekshe Tsomo.

Finally, the path is not a prescribed set of rules that we must learn to follow. Instead, it encourages us to question what we've been taught and decide for ourselves what is reasonable and good. As the Buddha said:

> Do not believe in anything simply because you have
> heard it. Do not believe in anything simply because
> it is spoken and rumored by many. Do not believe
> in anything simply because it is found written in
> your religious books. Do not believe in anything
> merely on the authority of your teachers and elders.
> Do not believe in traditions because they have been
> handed down for many generations. But after ob-
> servation and analysis, when you find that anything
> agrees with reason and is conducive to the good and
> benefit of one and all, then accept and live up to it.

Far from being a mysterious or inaccessible belief system, the Eightfold Path presents a clear set of moral principles that can be applied to everyday life. Buddhists follow the path as a way to achieve enlightenment. Others use it as a tool to support moral growth or spiritual practices including Twelve Step recovery.

Sometimes, using the path is as simple as reminding ourselves to be present, to act honorably, to practice compassion, and to strive for wisdom.

> **PRACTICE: Seeds of change.** When we practice the Eightfold Path (or any self-improvement program, for that matter), changing our thoughts and behaviors takes time and patience. Try planting and tending actual seeds or bulbs to remind yourself of this truth. Marigolds, coleus, and paperwhite narcissus are popular choices for indoor gardeners, while outdoor gardeners have a vast array of options.
>
> The focus is not so much on *what* we're growing as on the growing process itself: preparing, planting, tending, observing, nurturing, and patiently waiting for the transformation that nature inevitably brings. *What seeds of change have you planted in yourself?*

Freedom through Self-Discipline

"No person is free who is not master of himself," wrote Epictetus almost two thousand years ago. It's a principle that echoes through many cultural traditions, including Buddhism and Christianity. After all, self-discipline is the quality that enables us to resist harmful temptations and persist in our efforts to build a more virtuous, more satisfying life.

But many of us who have struggled with problematic behaviors have had a shaky relationship with self-discipline. Most compulsions and addictions begin with the desire for instant gratification. They deepen as we lose control over our behavior, a characteristic that is spelled out in the First Step: "We admitted we were powerless over alcohol—that our lives had become unmanageable."

In recovery, we soon discover that self-discipline is essential to our sobriety—both physical *and* emotional. But we also learn that willpower alone is not enough. What is sometimes called "white-knuckle sobriety"—a grim sort of "pull yourself up by your own bootstraps" approach—can result in a prolonged period of joyless abstinence or even relapse. So what is the legitimate role of self-discipline in recovery, and how can it lead to a happier way of life?

To begin, it helps to understand what self-discipline is and is not. Willpower and self-discipline are closely related, but there's a key difference between them. Willpower is the forceful, determined effort to overcome an obstacle or accomplish a goal. Because it requires a great deal of mental energy, it is almost always a short-term strategy.

Studies suggest that willpower is a limited resource that can be depleted. Most of us simply can't sustain the energy required to impose our will on a long-term basis. This explains why, if we're trying to lose weight, we might be able to say no to a stack of pancakes for breakfast but find ourselves eating a quart of ice cream that night. Our supply of willpower has actually run out.

Self-discipline, on the other hand, is a habitual, sustainable strategy for living in harmony with our values and achieving our goals. When we have self-discipline, we're able to delay gratification and override unskillful thoughts or impulses. Through awareness and commitment to our own well-being, we're able not only to resist the stack of pancakes but to forgo the ice cream later on—with little sense of deprivation.

That's because at its core, "self-discipline is self-caring," in the words of author M. Scott Peck. He contends that when we value our self, we favor behaviors that help us and try to avoid those that hurt us. Thus, if we're trying to lose weight, the reward of eating ice cream would pale in comparison to the reward of taking care of our health.

"[W]hen one considers oneself valuable, one will take care of oneself in all ways that are necessary," observes Peck. Discipline, then, is not a form of punishment or deprivation. Instead, it is the ultimate expression of belief in our own worth.

Many people associate a lack of self-discipline with fun, spontaneity, and freedom. And it's true that acting on a playful impulse can sometimes produce joyful moments. But as thrilling as they are, those moments are fleeting and have little to do with our overall happiness.

Indeed, research has shown that a habitual lack of self-discipline is the underlying *cause* of many individual and societal problems, "including unhealthy eating, lack of exercising, academic failure and underachievement, procrastination, substance abuse, impulse buying, and delinquent behavior," said one study. The same study revealed that high self-discipline is associated with high levels of personal happiness, noting: "Feeling good rather than bad may be a core benefit of having good self-control, and being well satisfied with life is an important consequence . . . High self-control does make you happy."

To put it another way, we create long-term contentment not by indulging our whims and impulses, but by conducting our day-to-day life in ways that align with our goals and values. Of course, this doesn't mean that we should adopt a rigid approach to life! Too much discipline can lead to joylessness, just as too little can create misery. The goal is to strike an optimal balance, what Aristotle called the golden mean and the Buddha called the middle way. Self-discipline requires awareness, intention, and effort—but it also requires openness, judgment, and flexibility.

It's worth noting that research has found that self-discipline seems to have a genetic component. Some of us may be born with a stronger inclination for it than others. (I saw this in my own children, who from an early age differed considerably in their ability to regulate their behavior.) Nevertheless, we all have the capacity to improve our self-discipline. Meditation and mindfulness are proven tools for doing just that.

As with any skill, the more we practice, the better we get at it. By marshalling our energies in service of our goals and values, self-discipline becomes not a chore, but rather a path to a happier, more satisfying life. The Dalai Lama expressed this idea succinctly: "A disciplined mind leads to happiness, and an undisciplined mind leads to suffering."

PRACTICE: **The power of om.** *Om* is a Sanskrit word that blends mind, body, and spirit. To practice this well-known meditation, begin by sitting in a comfortable position, hands resting palms-up in your lap. You may close your eyes or keep them open. Breathe normally.

When you are ready, take a deep, full breath, filling your lungs and expanding your stomach. As you exhale say the word *om* quietly and gently. Blend the sounds and extend them as long as you can naturally and without force. Repeat this process, breathing deeply and saying "om" on each exhalation. Notice how the sound originates from your intention (mind). Feel the vibration in your throat and chest cavity (body). Notice the stillness from which it arises and into which it goes (spirit).

Continue to focus on the perfect quality of om, saying it calmly and gently throughout your practice. *What does the sound of om feel like to you?*

What about Karma?

"What you do is what happens to you," my yoga teacher sometimes reminds us at the end of class. It's her version of the well-known saying "What goes around comes around"—which is itself a kind of shorthand for the law of karma.

While karma is associated with the idea of reincarnation in Buddhism and other Eastern religions, it more generally refers to the principle of cause and effect: good deeds create good karma and future happiness, and bad deeds create the opposite. This theory, while hardly a scientific fact, aligns with the views of philosophers and social scientists who contend that people who live moral lives tend to be happier than those who don't.

Buddhists are quick to point out that karma should not be confused with reward and punishment. In keeping with the principle of nonjudgment, it's a neutral, natural law of action and reaction, of behavior and consequence. In fact, the original meaning of *karma* is "action." From this comes the understanding that our actions, including our intention behind them, determine what happens to us.

Skillful actions flow from mindfulness, generosity, honesty, and compassion. Unskillful actions come from delusion, selfishness, dishonesty, and hatred. Because the karmic energy we release into the world inevitably comes back to us, Buddhists believe, they place a strong emphasis on consciously controlling our thoughts and behavior. In the Buddha's words, "To enjoy good health, to bring true happiness to one's family, to bring peace to all, one must first control one's mind."

According to karmic law, then, self-discipline is the foundation of moral behavior, which in turn brings happiness. But what about the injustices that abound all around us? What about selfish and dishonest people who seem to prosper and thrive, or honest and generous people who suffer hardship and sorrow? What about victims of wars and other disasters? What's the role of karma then?

It's a question that brings us back to the Buddhist principle that pain is an inevitable part of the human experience, one that we must learn to accept in order to grow. M. Scott Peck echoes that idea in the opening lines of *The Road Less Traveled*:

> Life is difficult. This is a great truth, one of the greatest truths. It is a great truth because once we truly see this truth, we transcend it. Once we truly know that life is difficult—once we truly understand and accept it—then life is no longer difficult. Because once it is accepted, the fact that life is difficult no longer matters . . . It is only because of problems that we grow mentally and spiritually.

The point he makes is not that suffering is unimportant. It's that suffering is a normal part of life, not only inevitable but also essential for personal growth. Karmic law does not protect us from this fundamental truth. We get karma wrong when we think of it as a kind of cosmic justice system that doles out rewards and punishments according to our merit. In reality, injustice persists, life is hard, and heartache and hardship befall the virtuous just as they do the wicked. We have little control over these things. What we *do* have control over is our behavior.

In the Buddhist view of things, we are all products of our karmic "conditioning." That is, our character is shaped by our moral actions. This important concept is worth repeating: *Our character is shaped by our moral actions.*

We tend to assume that it's the other way around—that people with "bad" character do bad things while people with "good" character do good things. But the truth is that we all have positive and negative traits. Our habits—our habitual thoughts and actions, whether good or bad—determine which traits become magnified over time and which fall away. That which we repeatedly do eventually becomes second nature. Every action we take molds our character, which creates our karmic energy.

It is within our power to control our actions and to choose a better path no matter how unfamiliar it may be. The Twelve Step slogan "Fake it till you make it" gets at this truth—that when our actions come first, our heart and mind will follow.

In practical terms, good karma doesn't protect us from suffering or reward us with perpetual bliss. Karma simply reflects back to us the good (or ill) that we have put into the world. When we practice mindfulness, self-discipline, integrity, and compassion—in short, when we strive for moral goodness—we nurture the best within our self and choose a path to a more satisfying life. In the words of the Roman emperor Marcus Aurelius: "The happiness of your life depends upon the quality of your thoughts: therefore, guard accordingly, and take care that you entertain no notions unsuitable to virtue and reasonable nature."

> **REFLECTION:** "Each person has inside a basic decency and goodness," wrote the cellist Pablo Casals. "If he listens to it and acts on it, he is giving a great deal of what it is the world needs most. It is not complicated but it takes courage. It takes courage for a person to listen to his own good." *What steps can you take to listen to and act on your inner "decency and goodness"?*

●

An Illuminated Life

No man is an island,
Entire of itself,
Every man is a piece of the continent,
A part of the main.

If a clod be washed away by the sea,
Europe is the less,
As well as if a promontory were,
As well as if a manor of thy friend's
Or of thine own were:
Any man's death diminishes me,
Because I am involved in mankind,
And therefore never send to know for whom the bell tolls;
It tolls for thee.

—John Donne

IN A WELL-KNOWN PASSAGE from Ernest Hemingway's novel *The Sun Also Rises,* the world-weary Lady Ashley shares her personal moral philosophy with her friend Jake:

> "You know it makes one feel rather good deciding not to be a bitch."
>
> "Yes."
>
> "It's sort of what we have instead of God."
>
> "Some people have God," I said. "Quite a lot."
>
> "He never worked very well with me."

For Lady Ashley, "not being a bitch" is a kind of shorthand for moral goodness, the principle she relies on to guide her through life's struggles. In a way, she's defining her "higher power," something each of us is called to do on our journey of recovery.

A Power Greater Than Ourselves

Whether we follow a Twelve Step program or choose another path to personal growth, a belief in *something* beyond the confines of our own narrow existence is an essential part of healing from addictions of all kinds and forms. This principle has been a cornerstone of AA since its founding, growing out of Carl Jung's advice to an alcoholic patient that his only hope for a cure was a "vital spiritual experience."

As Jung explained in a letter to Bill Wilson: "His craving for alcohol was the equivalent on a low level of the spiritual thirst of our being for wholeness, expressed in mediaeval language: the union with God . . . You see, Alcohol in Latin is 'spiritus' and you use the same word for the highest religious experience as well as for the most depraving poison. The helpful formula therefore is: spiritus contra spiritum."

That well-known final phrase—loosely meaning that spiritual awakening counters the spiritual withering of addiction—embodies Jung's belief that all humans long for spiritual wholeness, for a sense of belonging to something bigger than themselves. If our life lacks sufficient meaning, if we are confined to "too narrow a spiritual horizon," in Jung's words, we turn to addiction or other self-destructive behaviors to fill the void.

Step Two captures this concept succinctly: "Came to believe that a Power greater than ourselves could restore us to sanity." But what exactly is that greater power, and what role does it play in our daily life?

Those questions get to the heart of our search for meaning.

∗

Every known civilization has created mythologies and rituals to bridge the gulf between the material world and the mysterious unknown. Prehistoric goddess figures, elaborate ancient burial sites, the pyramids, Stonehenge, the great cathedrals—even today's space programs—all attest to the human longing to connect with "something more."

For people in recovery, that longing must be answered if we are to fully heal. Most of us can remember an intense inner emptiness that existed long before our self-destructive behaviors took hold. For months, years, or even decades, we filled that emptiness with addictive substances or mind-numbing behaviors. We deadened our feelings and denied the existence of our lost and hurting self. In the process, we forgot how to hope or trust or believe in much of anything.

Now, free of the delusions of addiction, we come face-to-face with our inner need. Some of us find answers in religious faith. The phrase "my higher power whom I choose to call God" is heard frequently in Twelve Step meetings. Others define their higher power as love of family, service to others, or—like Lady Ashley—moral goodness. Still others find it in creative expression or connection with the natural world.

However we define our higher power, it awakens something vital within us—call it heart, soul, spirit, or simply a higher level of understanding. It "restores us to sanity" not only by freeing us from the distorted thinking of addiction, but by opening our eyes to the higher nature of our own existence.

So much of our life is consumed by trivial concerns and petty grievances that we tend to forget that our time on this planet is short, that life is fragile, and that we are interconnected with all living beings. We measure out our life in coffee spoons, to paraphrase T. S. Eliot, and lose sight of the things that matter most.

Our higher power, whether it's a presence or an ideal, reminds us of life's deeper truths. It connects us with our core values and guides us toward moral goodness. Sometimes, in moments of grace, our higher power reveals to us the transcendent and eternal within our self. The poet Walt Whitman captured something of the joy of this experience in the following lines:

> I inhale great draughts of space;
> The east and the west are mine, and the north
>   and the south are mine.

I am larger, better than I thought;
I did not know I held so much goodness.

REFLECTION: "Whatever precious jewel there is in the heavenly worlds, there is nothing comparable to one who is awakened," wrote the Buddha. *How can you awaken to your higher power today?*

The Illusion of Separateness

"A human being is a part of the whole, called by us 'Universe,' a part limited in time and space," Albert Einstein wrote in a letter to a friend. He continued:

> He experiences himself, his thoughts and feelings as something separated from the rest—a kind of optical delusion of his consciousness. This delusion is a kind of prison for us, restricting us to our personal desires and to affection for a few persons nearest to us. Our task must be to free ourselves from this prison by widening our circle of compassion to embrace all living creatures and the whole of nature in its beauty. Nobody is able to achieve this completely, but the striving for such achievement is in itself a part of the liberation and a foundation for inner security.

Einstein's words—distinctly Buddhist in tone—reveal his belief that our painful sense of separateness is the result of our misperceptions about the nature of existence. We experience ourselves as singular and distinct from everyone else, but in reality, we are all part of a greater whole.

The message harkens to the Renaissance poet John Donne's well-known declaration that "No man is an island." The sentiment goes far beyond mere poetry. For scientists now know that everything in the universe—from the tiniest speck of dust to the most dazzling stars—is interrelated.

※

"We are stardust. We are golden," wrote the singer-songwriter Joni Mitchell in 1969. She was right. There are only around one hundred known elements—the building blocks of matter—in the entire universe. Science has shown that we humans are literally made of stardust, elements thrown off by dying stars or stellar explosions. In fact, we carry material in our body that is as old as the universe itself. When we gaze in wonder at the stars, we are seeing the very stuff of which we are made.

Still, the mind-bending reality of our physical connectedness to the universe does little to alter our perception of self as something unique. And this is not necessarily a bad thing. After all, developing our interests, talents, and values—the very qualities that make us uniquely who we are—involves paying attention to how we are different from others and learning to listen to our own inner voice.

But our sense of individual personhood can leave us feeling lonely and disconnected, struggling with feelings of separateness that, in Einstein's words, can seem like a "prison." The human need for connection is so fundamental that "loneliness is the first thing which God's eye named not good," the poet John Milton observed more than four hundred years ago. He was referring to the Bible's book of Genesis, in which God says of Adam, "It is not good for the man to be alone. I will make him a helper."

Of course, being alone and being lonely are two different things. It's entirely possible to be content in solitude, just as it's possible to be lonely in a crowd. It all depends on how we understand our self in relation to the world around us.

For many of us in recovery, addiction went hand-in-hand with emotional isolation. We built walls to protect ourselves from anyone who dared to challenge our self-destructive path. We numbed our feelings as the losses mounted. We came to see ourselves as outsiders and operated on the belief that we were fundamentally different from everyone else.

Unfortunately, feelings of not belonging can linger even in recovery, especially when we interact with people whose personal history may be different from our own. I once heard a woman at an AA meeting say that when she first got sober, she had no idea how to deal with "normal" people. "I tried to copy the way they dressed and talked, but I felt like a fraud," she said. "I couldn't relate to them and they sure as hell wouldn't have been able to relate to me if they'd known my story."

What she failed to realize was that her fear of being judged had led her to judge others without really knowing their beliefs, attitudes, and life stories. Who knows what connections might have resulted—what bridges might have been built—had she been able to approach the situation with an open mind? But this kind of "us and them" thinking is common—not only in the recovery community but throughout society. We zero in on apparent differences, impose instant labels, and make assumptions about whether we have anything in common with others. As a result, we build walls instead of bridges and reinforce our sense of being separate.

Yet all around us there are powerful reminders that our similarities are much greater than our differences. When we share an exhilarating moment with strangers at a concert or sporting event, help disaster victims we don't know, rescue someone in danger, or volunteer for a cause, we don't consider skin color or religious beliefs or any of the myriad other distinctions that distract and divide us. Instead, we respond instinctively to a fundamental truth: we are all connected, each to other, by our common humanity.

It's by carrying that recognition into our daily life that we can begin to expand our "circle of compassion," as Einstein advised. When we remind ourselves that everyone we encounter has hopes and dreams, is vulnerable to pain, and struggles in this journey of life—just like us—our compassionate awareness strengthens the bonds that connect us all.

> **PRACTICE: Cherish all beings.** The Dalai Lama wrote, "As you breathe in, cherish yourself. As you breathe out, cherish all beings." In this focused meditation, we'll use these thoughts as a mantra. Get into a comfortable position, either sitting or lying down. Take a moment to check in with your body, noting any areas of discomfort and adjusting your position as necessary. Take two or three cleansing breaths. When you are ready, breathe in and say to yourself, "I cherish myself." As you breathe out, say softly, "I cherish all beings." Repeat these phrases calmly and softly for five or ten minutes.
>
> Allow yourself to be soothed by the rhythm of your breath. Pay attention to the meaning of your words. If distracting

thoughts enter your mind, acknowledge them without judgment and let them drift away. *How can you plant seeds of connection within yourself so they will take root and blossom?*

The Eternal in the Here and Now

What was your face before you were born?

This cryptic question—a well-known Zen koan (a question that defies rational answers)—is meant to challenge the way we typically think about time and self. Since our concept of time has a subtle but important impact on how we understand our self, it's a topic well worth considering.

Most of us are used to thinking about time in a linear way— that is, as a chain of events progressing from the past into the future. Like the biblical narrative that begins with the Creation and ends with the Last Judgment, Western tradition envisions time as one-directional, with each moment different from what went before and no repetition.

But in the ancient world, and in many indigenous traditions, time is cyclical, mirroring the seasons of the natural world in a repeating pattern of birth, life, death, and rebirth. Buddhism, along with many other Eastern traditions, incorporates the idea of repetition into its concept of time. Because everything is cyclical with no definitive endpoint, eternity itself takes on an immediacy that is not present in Western thought. The author Diane Morgan explained the differences this way:

> In the West, time is often compared to a swift-running river. It flows in one direction—toward eternity. This viewpoint makes us look at eternity

in a one-sided way. Eternity lies in the future; it's
something that awaits us . . . We don't care where
the river springs from; we're not much interested
in our past.

Although many Westerners spend a considerable amount of
time contemplating a life after death, life before birth is left out
of the equation. We don't know, and we don't care. In the East,
however, time is more aptly compared to a great primeval ocean,
always existing, totally surrounding us. It's our source and our
destination. Eternity doesn't await us, for we are present in it right
now.

A linear view of time is very efficient in promoting the belief
that we can make progress and that tomorrow can be better than
today (the stuff of which self-help books are made!). But it can
also lead to a certain level of anxiety, an uneasy feeling that time is
running out like sand through an hourglass. Ironically, this sense
of urgency does little to make us appreciate the time we have. Instead, we feel compelled to *do,* to hurry, to multitask, to get things
done—and in the process miss out on the very essence of our own
existence.

If we shift our perspective just a little, we begin to see that
while our mortal journey is indeed limited by time and space, our
essential being is part of all eternity. Just as "we belong to each
other," as Mother Teresa said, we also belong to the stars and the
sky and the infinite wonders of the universe. Paradoxically, we per-
ceive this truth only when we learn to slow down and focus on the
present moment.

Only then is our mind free to explore, expand, and open to the everlasting nature of reality. Thoreau, who understood this as well as anyone, wrote: "Time is but the stream I go a-fishing in. I drink at it; but while I drink I see the sandy bottom and detect how shallow it is. Its thin current slides away, but eternity remains."

> **PRACTICE: What are you doing?** One way to awaken to the present moment is through a form of meditation called daily life practice meditation. In this practice, we focus our attention on a common activity. Instead of letting our mind drift away while our hands or feet do the work, we consciously engage our senses with whatever we're doing.
>
> Folding the laundry is a good activity for practice. Remove some freshly laundered items from the line or dryer and form a loose pile. Take a moment to observe the various colors and textures of the fabrics. Inhale the scent, paying attention to its complex elements. Then, as you select an item from the pile, notice how it feels in your hands. Feel the sensation of flesh on fabric as you smooth out the wrinkles. Watch your fingers work as you fold the item into the desired shape and size. Continue in this fashion, taking your time, really seeing, smelling, and feeling the task of folding the laundry.
>
> This type of meditation can be done almost anywhere: while taking a shower, washing the dishes, preparing or eating a meal, walking to or from your car—the possibilities are endless. *What's your favorite way to engage your senses as you practice being in the moment?*

Having Had a Spiritual Awakening

"Know thyself." This simple maxim has been enshrined as a foundation of wisdom since time immemorial. Carved into the ancient Greek Temple of Apollo at Delphi, it's an abbreviated form of an even older Egyptian proverb: "Man, know thyself, and you are going to know the gods."

However we conceive of God, the universal, or the everlasting, the ancient Egyptians believed that it exists within each of us. While this may seem like an extravagant claim, writers and philosophers throughout the ages have concurred.

The Buddha said, "To attain enlightenment without seeing your nature is impossible." The apostle Luke quoted Jesus as saying, "Neither shall they say, Lo here! or, lo there! for, behold, the kingdom of God is within you." Ralph Waldo Emerson wrote, "If thou canst bear strong meat of simple truth . . . Then take this fact unto thy soul, God dwells in thee."

And Alcoholics Anonymous teaches that recovery leads to an awakening of our spiritual core. In particular, Step Twelve—"Having had a spiritual awakening as a result of these steps"—speaks of a spiritual essence within our self. This Step reminds us that we grow spiritually not only by looking outward, but also by awakening what's already inside us.

These diverse strains of philosophy contain a common theme, that we are fundamentally spiritual beings. As the French philosopher Pierre Teilhard de Chardin famously said, "We are not human beings having a spiritual experience. We are spiritual beings having a human experience." To put it another way, we all carry within us something of the transcendent and eternal. In the busyness of everyday life, it's easy to ignore this truth. But when we neglect our spiritual core, we diminish our experience of life itself and dim our own inner light.

The practice of mindfulness teaches us to slow down and re-kindle that light. We learn to attend to our thoughts, feelings, attitudes, and beliefs. We nurture the inner goodness that sustains and inspires us. And we awaken to the sublime within our self.

> REFLECTION: "The door is wide and open. Don't go back to sleep," wrote the thirteenth century Persian poet Rumi. *How can you awaken your spirit today?*

Rediscovering Joy

"The highest point a man can attain is not Knowledge, or Virtue, or Goodness, or Victory, but something even greater, more heroic and more despairing: Sacred Awe!"

There was a time in my life when those words from the author Nikos Kazantzakis would have held little meaning for me. As a case in point, I remember visiting Yellowstone National Park with my husband and children many years ago. My marriage was crumbling. I was deeply depressed and drinking heavily. I was so blinded by misery that the spectacular beauty of Yellowstone—or anyplace else, for that matter—meant nothing to me.

Fortunately, I had an opportunity to return to Yellowstone years later. It was as if I were seeing the place for the first time—which, in a sense, I was. The incredible wildlife, the otherworldly thermal basins, the sprawling grasslands and winding rivers and soaring mountains—I found all of it profoundly moving. Time and again I experienced a sense of something timeless, serene, majestic, almost holy—in truth, a sense of "sacred awe."

What made the difference? On the second trip, I was awake.

"The difference between misery and happiness depends on what we do with our attention," wrote Sharon Salzberg. Her point is that in any given situation, we have a choice of what to focus on. On my first Yellowstone visit, my focus was on my failing marriage. On my second, I was focused on the visual and spiritual experience.

To be fair, I was in an emotional crisis the first time around. When we're facing a crisis, we usually don't feel like we have a choice about where to put our attention. It gets consumed by the problem at hand, and it's hard to think about anything else. And certainly, when something requires immediate attention, common sense says that we should attend to it.

Still, there's a difference between dealing with a problem and endlessly agonizing about it. What did I gain by fretting about the state of my marriage and ignoring the splendors of the park? Nothing but an unmitigated deluge of misery. My attachment to my pain only made a difficult situation worse.

One of the most valuable skills we gain from mindfulness is the ability to live in the moment. For it's startling but true that we can feel happiness even in the midst of difficulties. The trick is to consciously turn our attention to whatever it is—nature, family, music, art, literature, prayer, meditation—that nurtures our spirit.

Practicing gratitude can help us do just that.

I once knew a frail, elderly woman whose appreciation for life made a lasting impression on me. She was a childless widow who lived in a tiny apartment on the eighth floor of a public housing complex. She'd survived abuse by her stepmother and first husband and endured the death of her beloved second husband.

After working in factories most of her life, she possessed no material wealth. But she was rich in spirit and found pleasure in the smallest things right up to the end.

One memory in particular stands out. I had picked her up to take her grocery shopping. After helping her to my car and putting her walker in the back seat, I carefully backed out of the parking lot. She turned to me with a big smile.

"I had a grand time last night," she said, her eyes sparkling behind her thick glasses. "I had some root beer in my fridge and a man down the hall had some ice cream. So a bunch of us pulled our chairs into the hallway and we made root beer floats. We had ourselves a party."

The incident was typical of her deep and abiding knack for appreciating the "little" things in life. She instinctively knew, as Jon Kabat-Zinn has pointed out, that "The little things? The little moments? They aren't little." She was blessed with the gift of gratitude, which made an otherwise difficult life a thing of beauty. There is much to be learned from her example.

When we choose to appreciate what is good and lovely even in the midst of hardship, we're not donning rose-tinted glasses or retreating to a state of denial. We're simply opening our eyes to a wider reality—one that embraces life in all its complexities, its harshness and beauty, its tears and laughter, its sorrow and joy.

Some of us in recovery may fear that our capacity for joy has been destroyed by the harmful effects of addiction. And it's true that some substances have been shown to damage the brain's natural reward center, limiting our ability to feel pleasure. But science has also revealed the brain's marvelous capacity to heal itself and to generate new neural pathways. We can literally rewire our brain in positive ways through conscious behavioral choices, including the practice of mindfulness and meditation.

When we teach our self to awaken, our life is transformed in unimaginable ways. We begin to let go of the fears and misperceptions that prevent us from living a full and satisfying life. We nurture an attitude of compassionate awareness that strengthens our bond to all beings. We understand our self and others as part of the eternal cycle of birth, growth, decline, transformation, and rebirth.

And by truly knowing our self in all the infinite richness of what it means to be human, we open our heart to the joy of emotional and spiritual wholeness. In the words of the poet Max Ehrmann:

> You are a child of the universe,
> no less than the trees and the stars;
> you have a right to be here.
> And whether or not it is clear to you,
> no doubt the universe is unfolding as it should.

REFLECTION: "I got up early and bathed in the pond; that was a religious exercise, and one of the best things which I did. They say that characters were engraven on the bathing tub of King Tching-thang to this effect: 'Renew thyself completely each day; do it again, and again, and forever again.'" These words from Thoreau remind us that every day brings an opportunity to start again. *What can you do to renew yourself "again, and again, and forever again"?*

●

Lightening Up

Listen to the inner light; it will guide you.
Listen to the inner peace; it will feed you.
Listen to the inner love; it will transform you.

—Sri Chinmoy

For years, I had a spotty relationship with mindfulness. I'm impatient by nature, and all that talk of "slowing down" and "paying attention" made me antsy. Still, something about the concept intrigued me, so every now and then I'd try a yoga class, a meditation session—even an occasional weekend retreat.

I didn't stick with anything very long, but some glimmers of mindfulness must have seeped in—enough, anyway, to sustain me at a very difficult moment. At that time, I was struggling to support myself as a freelance writer. I'd applied for a temporary position as a writer-researcher at a historical association—a prospect that absolutely thrilled me—and I'd convinced myself that I was sure to get the job. After all, I was well qualified, enthusiastic, and willing to work for next to nothing.

After waiting on pins and needles for what felt like an eternity, I got a letter in the mail. It was one of those polite little letters that talk about impressive qualifications, a talented applicant pool, a difficult decision . . . the bottom line was they'd chosen someone else.

I remember a peculiar stillness coming over me. I had no idea what I was going to do or how I was even going to pay the next month's rent. But instead of crying or panicking, I sank into a seated meditation position on my living-room floor, closed my eyes, and began to focus on my breath. One thought became my mantra: let me learn to accept this.

I have no idea how long I sat there. But in time, a feeling of peace came over me. And life did go on.

Since then, I've made meditation a part of my daily routine. It calms me and centers me and reminds me to try to be a better person. It also inspired me to write this book.

For those of us who have been touched by addiction in *any* way, mindfulness offers a gentle, practical path to growth and healing. It helps us discover inner strengths and build the skills we need for greater contentment and peace of mind. Mindfulness can even bring happiness much closer to hand.

Still, becoming more mindful won't automatically solve all our problems or instantly turn us into better versions of ourselves. It won't dramatically change our life. At least, not at first. Like recovery itself, the rewards of mindfulness come gradually, the cumulative effects of small steps taken one day at a time, sometimes one minute at a time—until mindfulness becomes not only a practice but a way of life.

Becoming more mindful need not be complicated or time consuming. For some of us, practicing mindfulness can be as simple as remembering to focus on the breath periodically throughout the day. Others may choose to commit to regular meditation, prayer, or other contemplative practice, while others practice mindfulness through activities such as painting, gardening, journaling, jogging, or yoga. And many of us find that a combination of approaches is most rewarding.

However we choose to *practice* mindfulness, its core principles remain the same:

Being present: Paying attention to where we are, what we're doing, and what we're thinking.

Practicing compassion: Extending tolerance, empathy, kindness, and forgiveness to others and ourselves.

Letting go: Accepting that change is the natural order of existence and that neither pain nor pleasure lasts forever.

Cultivating a spiritual practice: Setting aside unplugged, restorative time for contemplation, connection, and moments of calm.

When we are guided by these principles—and forgive ourselves when we fall short (think progress, not perfection)—our heart and mind begin to expand in unexpected ways. We awaken to a truer understanding of who we really are, what actually matters to us, and how we intend to spend our precious time on this beautiful planet.

Best of all, when we deepen our recovery through the practice of mindfulness, we begin to be guided by the pure, abiding truth of our own inner light.

ACKNOWLEDGMENTS

I am deeply grateful to the many people who were instrumental in the development of this book. Vanessa Torrado believed in and championed the manuscript from the start. Her unflagging encouragement and kind, insightful guidance were indispensable. Mindy Keskinen provided thoughtful and sensitive editing throughout the writing process—and came up with the perfect title. The editorial and design services team at Hazelden, including Jean Cook and Betty Christiansen, paid scrupulous attention to detail, and Terri Kinne's design work was nothing short of inspired. To all—and to the many teachers who have lightened my path along the way—thank you.

RESOURCES

Here are some resources that informed this book, which you may want to explore for further information:

ONLINE RESOURCES

- A View on Buddhism, http://www.viewonbuddhism.org
- *InnerSelf,* Innerself.com
- *Lion's Roar: Buddhist Wisdom for Our Time,* https://www.lionsroar.com
- The On Being Project, https://onbeing.org
- *The Virtue Blog,* https://thevirtueblog.com

BOOKS

- *A Return to Love: Reflections on the Principles of A Course in Miracles* by Marianne Williamson, New York: HarperOne Reissue Edition, 1996
- *The Road Less Traveled* by M. Scott Peck, New York: Touchstone, 1978
- *Real Happiness: The Power of Meditation* by Sharon Salzberg, New York: Workman Publishing, 2011
- *Walden* by Henry David Thoreau, Los Angeles: Empire Books, [1854] 2012
- *Wherever You Go, There You Are* by Jon Kabat-Zinn, New York: Hyperion, 1994
- *The Wise Heart: A Guide to the Universal Teachings of Buddhist Psychology* by Jack Kornfield, New York: Bantam Reprint Edition, 2009

CHAPTER 1

12 ***Papa, at the head of the table:*** Leo Buscaglia, *Papa, My Father: A Celebration of Dads,* Thorofare, NJ: Slack, 1989.

18 ***One study concluded:*** Markus MacGill, "Meditation Has 'Some Benefit against Anxiety, Depression and Pain,'" *Medical News Today,* January 7, 2014, https://www.medicalnewstoday.com /articles/270824.php.

18 ***Neuroscientist Richard Davidson:*** Richard Davidson, PhD, "Investigating Healthy Minds," aired June 23, 2011, *On Being with Krista Tippett,* updated June 14, 2012, https://onbeing.org /programs/richard-davidson-investigating-healthy-minds/.

24 ***Western religion conceives:*** Diane Morgan, "Bridging East & West Religions and Beliefs," *InnerSelf,* http://www.innerself.com /spirituality/bridging.htm.

CHAPTER 2

29 ***When I heard the learn'd astronomer:*** Walt Whitman, *Leaves of Grass,* "When I Heard the Learn'd Astronomer," Philadelphia: David McKay, [c1900], Bartleby.com, 1999, www.bartleby. com/142/.

31 ***Research suggests that we have:*** "How Many Thoughts Do We Have per Minute?" Reference.com, https://www.reference.com /world-view/many-thoughts-per-minute-cb7fcf22ebbf8466.

39 ***A well-known study:*** Brigham and Women's Hospital, "If You're Not Looking for It, You Probably Won't See It," *ScienceDaily,* July 19, 2013, www.sciencedaily.com/releases/2013/07 /130719112134.htm.

47 ***An article in the* Harvard Business Review:** Jeanine Prime and Elizabeth Salib, "The Best Leaders Are Humble Leaders," *Harvard Business Review,* May 12, 2014, https://hbr.org/2014/05/the-best -leaders-are-humble-leaders.

48 *Be patient toward all that is unsolved:* Maria Rilke Rainer, *Letters to a Young Poet*, New York: Vintage, 1986.

CHAPTER 3

54 *I think that that's a very different conception:* Richard Davidson, PhD, "Investigating Healthy Minds," aired June 23, 2011, *On Being with Krista Tippett,* updated June 14, 2012, https://onbeing.org /programs/richard-davidson-investigating-healthy-minds/.

61 *A group of fifth graders:* Patricia Leigh Brown, "In the Classroom, a New Focus on Quieting the Mind," *New York Times,* June 16, 2007, http://www.nytimes.com/2007/06/16/us/16mindful.html.

65 *What happens is of little significance:* Rabih Alameddine, *The Hakawati*, New York: Anchor Reprint Edition, 2009.

65 *According to professor Dan McAdams:* Emily Esfahani Smith, "The Two Kinds of Stories We Tell about Ourselves," TED Talk, January 12, 2017, https://ideas.ted.com/the-two-kinds-of-stories -we-tell-about-ourselves/.

67 *I never learned hate at home:* Dick Gregory with Robert Lipsyte, *Nigger: An Autobiography.* New York: Pocket, [1964] 1990.

68 *The author John Bradshaw explained:* John Bradshaw, quoted in AZ Quotes, http://www.azquotes.com/author/1787-John_Brad shaw.

70 *Just as pride means self-love:* James Gilligan, "Shame, Guilt, and Violence," *Social Research* 70, no. 4 (2003): 1149–180, http:// www.jstor.org/stable/40971965.

CHAPTER 4

77 *Suffering is a central theme:* Genesis 3:16, King James Bible online, https://www.kingjamesbibleonline.org.

77 *However, Christian doctrine does not teach:* Job 13:15, King James Bible online, https://www.kingjamesbibleonline.org.

80 *[W]e also glory in our sufferings:* Romans 5:3, Bible New International Version, https://www.bible.com/.

80 ***It is under the greatest adversity:*** The Dalai Lama quote is found in A View on Buddhism.org, http://www.viewonbuddhism.org /dharma-quotes-quotations-buddhist/obstacles-difficulties -problems-suffering-pain.htm.

86 ***Sometimes we think that to develop an open heart:*** Dalai Lama, quoted by Sharon Salzberg in A View on Buddhism, http:// www.viewonbuddhism.org/dharma-quotes-quotations-buddhist /compassion-loving-kindness.htm.

88 ***Nelson Mandela was once asked:*** "Forgiving the Unforgiven," *Zen Sense,* November 4, 2008, http://zen-sense.blogspot.com /2008/11/forgiving-unforgiven.html.

91 ***Listen. Slide the weight:*** Barbara Kingsolver, *The Poisonwood Bible,* New York: Harper Perennial Modern Classics Reissue edition, 2008.

92 ***Finish each day and be done with it:*** Quote taken from James Elliot Cabot's *A Memoir of Ralph Waldo Emerson,* https:// en.wikiquote.org/wiki/Talk:Ralph_Waldo_Emerson.

93 ***In one social psychology research review:*** Theodore A. Powers et al., "The Effects of Self-Criticism and Self-Oriented Perfectionism on Goal Pursuit," *Personality and Social Psychology Bulletin* 37, no. 7 (July 2011): 964–75, http://www.academia.edu/1201857 /The_Effects_of_Self-Criticism_and_Self-Oriented_Perfection ism_on_Goal_Pursuit.

93 ***In the words of Dr. Kristin Neff:*** Tara Parker-Pope, "Go Easy on Yourself, a New Wave of Research Urges," *New York Times,* February 28, 2011, https://well.blogs.nytimes.com/2011/02/28 /go-easy-on-yourself-a-new-wave-of-research-urges/.

94 ***For example, studies have shown:*** Alexandra Sifferlin, "Why Facebook Makes You Feel Bad About Yourself," *Time,* January 24, 2013, http://healthland.time.com/2013/01/24/why-facebook -makes-you-feel-bad-about-yourself/.

95 ***To test the effectiveness:*** S. Marshall et al., "Self-Compassion Protects Against the Negative Effects of Low Self-Esteem: A Longitudinal Study in a Large Adolescent Sample," *Personality and Individual Differences* 74 (February 2015): 116–21.

96 *It's time for us to put down:* Steven C. Hayes, "Is Self-Compassion More Important Than Self-Esteem?" *Psychology Today,* December 23, 2014, https://www.psychologytoday.com/blog/get-out-your -mind/201412/is-self-compassion-more-important-self-esteem.

CHAPTER 5

100 *As soon as it became light:* Llewelyn Wyn Griffith, quoted in "A Christmas Truce," *The Virtue Blog,* Dec. 26, 2015, https:// thevirtueblog.com/2015/12/.

102 *Your beliefs become your thoughts:* Mahatma Gandhi, quoted in Good Reads, http://www.goodreads.com/quotes/50584-your -beliefs-become-your-thoughts-your-thoughts-become-your -words.

103 *Henry David Thoreau, perhaps more than any other writer:* Thoreau Society Shop at Walden Pond, http://www.shopatwalden pond.org/category_s/110.htm.

105 *What de Waal calls the "pillars of morality":* Frans de Waal, "Moral Behavior in Animals," TED Talk, November 2011, https:// www.ted.com/talks/frans_de_waal_do_animals_have_morals.

106 *Many adults, to be sure:* Richard Weissbourd, "Moral Adults: Moral Children," *Psychology Today,* November 9, 2009, https:// www.psychologytoday.com/blog/the-parents-we-mean-be /200911/moral-adults-moral-children.

107 *Principles are to people:* Carlos Reyles quoted in "Our Values Shape our Character and Culture," *The Clemmer Group,* https:// www.clemmergroup.com/articles/values-shape-character-culture/.

110 *When making moral choices:* Barbara O'Brien, "Buddhism and Morality," Learn Religions, updated March 11, 2019, https:// www.learnreligions.com/buddhism-and-morality-449726.

110 *Do not believe in anything simply because:* The Buddha, quoted in "Buddha Quotes," Scribd, https://www.scribd.com/document /79969285/Buddha-Quotes.

112 **Studies suggest that willpower:** "Is Willpower a Limited Resource?" American Psychological Association, https://www.apa.org/helpcenter/willpower-limited-resource.pdf.

113 **Self-discipline is self-caring:** M. Scott Peck, *The Road Less Traveled,* New York: Touchstone, 1978.

113 **A habitual lack of self-discipline:** Wilhelm Hofmann et al., "Yes, but Are They Happy? Effects of Trait Self-Control on Affective Well-Being and Life Satisfaction," *Journal of Personality* 82, no. 4 (August 2014): 265–77.

CHAPTER 6

120 **You know it makes one feel rather good:** Ernest Hemingway, *The Sun Also Rises,* Three Novels, New York: Charles Scribner's Sons, 1962.

122 **I inhale great draughts of space:** Walt Whitman, *Leaves of Grass,* "Song of the Open Road," Philadelphia: David McKay, [c1900], Bartleby.com, 1999, www.bartleby.com/142/.

123 **A human being is a part:** Albert Einstein, letter written in 1950 and posted on Letters of Note, http://www.lettersofnote.com /2011/11/delusion.html.

127 **In the West, time is often compared:** Diane Morgan, "Bridging East & West Religions and Beliefs," *InnerSelf,* http://www.innerself .com/spirituality/bridging.htm.

134 **You are a child of the universe:** Max Ehrmann, "Desiderata," All Poetry, https://allpoetry.com/Desiderata—Words-for-Life.

135 **Listen to Inner light:** Sri Chinmoy, from Poem 528, *The Wings of Light, part 11,* Agni Press, 1974, https://www.srichinmoy library.com/wl_11.

ABOUT THE AUTHOR

Beverly Conyers, MA, is a writer and college English teacher who lives in New England. A respected voice in recovery and wellness, she is also the author of *Everything Changes, The Recovering Heart,* the acclaimed classic *Addict in the Family,* and the upcoming guided journal *Follow Your Light.*

"IF YOU ARE DEPRESSED,
you are living in the past.

IF YOU ARE ANXIOUS,
you are living in the future.

IF YOU ARE AT PEACE,
you are living in the present."

— LAO TZU

2

BEING PRESENT

Most of us who are in recovery have struggled to cope with certain areas of our life. Addiction—whether to substances or obsessive behaviors and unhealthy relationships—provided a ready means of escape. But a clouded mind is a crippled mind, unable to learn the skills that support mental and emotional well-being.

Mindfulness is the opposite of addiction. Instead of offering escape, it provides a gentle path to awareness. Its promise is that as awareness grows, so, too, does our ability to cope with problems and create a happier way of life. Addiction is about escaping reality. Mindfulness is the conscious decision to face reality—even when it's difficult.

PRACTICE: WRITE ABOUT A DIFFICULT SITUATION THAT YOU TRIED TO ESCAPE THROUGH DESTRUCTIVE BEHAVIORS. WHAT WAS GOING ON? WHAT WAS THE RESULT?

A SLOWLY AND REVERENTLY,
HE AXIS ON WHICH THE
VOLVES—SLOWLY. EVENLY,
G TOWARD THE FUTURE.
CTUAL MOMENT.
OMENT IS *life.*"

8

THOUGHT OR REALITY?

It's easy to confuse thoughts with reality. We do it all the time:

"I think she doesn't like me, so it must be true."

"I think I can't do something, so I won't even try."

"I think the world is full of danger, so I'll never leave my comfort zone."

The interesting thing about thoughts is that we hardly notice them—but they are the invisible hands that shape our world. Our decisions, actions, emotions, the way we see our self and others—everything comes from our thoughts. Learning to notice our thoughts as thoughts is a crucial step in personal growth.

PRACTICE: COMPLETE THE FOLLOWING SENTENCES WITH THE FIRST THOUGHTS THAT COME TO MIND. AFTER YOU HAVE FINISHED, CIRCLE EACH SENTENCE AS "DEFINITELY TRUE," "MAYBE SOMEWHAT TRUE," OR "JUST A THOUGHT."

People are mostly _____   TRUE   MAYBE   JUST A
                                                     TRUE   THOUGHT

The world is a _____   TRUE   MAYBE   JUST A
                                                  TRUE   THOUGHT

I don't have enough _____ place.   TRUE   MAYBE   JUST A
                                                     TRUE   THOUGHT

Most people think I'm _____   TRUE   MAYBE   JUST A
                                                        TRUE   THOUGHT

I will never have _____   TRUE   MAYBE   JUST A
                                                    TRUE   THOUGHT

About Hazelden Publishing

As part of the Hazelden Betty Ford Foundation, Hazelden Publishing offers both cutting-edge educational resources and inspirational books. Our print and digital works help guide individuals in treatment and recovery, and their loved ones. Professionals who work to prevent and treat addiction also turn to Hazelden Publishing for evidence-based curricula, digital content solutions, and videos for use in schools, treatment programs, correctional programs, and electronic health records systems. We also offer training for implementation of our curricula.

Through published and digital works, Hazelden Publishing extends the reach of healing and hope to individuals, families, and communities affected by addiction and related issues.

For more information about Hazelden publications,
please call **800-328-9000**
or visit us online at **hazelden.org/bookstore**.

OTHER TITLES BY BEVERLY CONYERS

Addict in the Family
Stories of Loss, Hope, and Recovery

With over 75,000 copies sold, *Addict in the Family* is a must-have, trusted resource for anyone coping with the addiction of a family member.

Revised and updated in 2015.
ISBN 978-1-56838-999-8
Order No. 1018, also available as an ebook

Everything Changes
Help for Families of Newly Recovering Addicts

A compassionate, user-friendly handbook for family and friends navigating the many challenges that come with a loved one's new-found sobriety.

ISBN 978-1-59285-697-8
Order No. 3807, also available as an ebook

The Recovering Heart
Emotional Sobriety for Women

Beverly Conyers, a prominent voice in recovery, uses personal stories and informed insight to guide you in achieving emotional sobriety by addressing behaviors and feelings unique to the female recovery experience.

ISBN 978-1-61649-437-7
Order No. 3969, also available as an ebook

To order these or other resources from Hazelden Publishing, call **800-328-9000** or visit **hazelden.org/bookstore.**

OTHER TITLES THAT MAY INTEREST YOU

A Kinder Voice
Releasing Your Inner Critics with Mindfulness Slogans
by THÉRÈSE JACOBS-STEWART

Combining thought-awareness, lovingkindness practice and mindfulness meditation, this simple, time-tested method can be used throughout the day to quiet your critical voices and ease the mind. Through short, accessible phrases, readers will learn to reorient thinking when their inner critic shows up.

ISBN 978-1-61649-639-5
Order No. 9798, also available as an ebook

Mindfulness and the 12 Steps
Living Recovery in the Present Moment
by THÉRÈSE JACOBS-STEWART

A fresh resource to help those in recovery from addiction find their own spiritual path through the Buddhist practice of mindfulness.

ISBN 978-1-59285-820-0
Order No. 2862, also available as an ebook

Meditations for Women

Each Day a New Beginning
Daily Meditations for Women
by KAREN CASEY

These meditations, one for each day of the year, speak to the common experience, shared struggles, and unique strengths of a woman, especially those seeking support and spiritual growth in recovery.

ISBN 978-0-89486-161-1
Order No. 1076, also available as an ebook

To order these or other resources from Hazelden Publishing, call **800-328-9000** or visit **hazelden.org/bookstore.**

OTHER TITLES THAT MAY INTEREST YOU

Meditation Trilogy for Men

Cornerstones

Daily Meditations for the Journey into Manhood and Recovery

by VICTOR LA CERVA, MD

We all need tools to help us fully embrace the new way of life made possible through recovery. Truly break the addiction cycle by uncovering the reasons for former dependencies and behaviors, discovering new perspectives, reshaping your sense of masculinity, and building the coping skills that support real physical and emotional sobriety.

ISBN 978-1-61649-762-0
Order No. 3518, also available as an ebook

Touchstones

A Book of Daily Meditations for Men

In the quest for sustained sobriety and self-development, we must look outside of ourselves to discover our inner truths. Whether we are facing dependency or parenthood, marriage or meditation, everyone needs a guide to embolden their coping skills and settle in to a better, more balanced life.

ISBN 978-0-89486-394-3
Order No. 5029, also available as an ebook

Stepping Stones

More Daily Meditations for Men

In the spiritual successor to the best-selling *Touchstones,* the author continues to explore masculinity and sobriety. Now well beyond recovery's trailhead, we confront life itself. *Stepping Stones* guides your self-help discovery along its next steps, ensuring your recovery finds inspiration, meaning, and brilliance.

ISBN 978-1-61649-828-3
Order No. 5859, also available as an ebook

To order these or other resources from Hazelden Publishing, call **800-328-9000** or visit **hazelden.org/bookstore.**